HOW TO BE A
PEACEFUL SCHOOL

of related interest

How to Create Kind Schools
12 extraordinary projects making schools
happier and helping every child fit in
Jenny Hulme
Foreword by Claude Knights, CEO of Kidscape
ISBN 978 1 84905 591 8
eISBN 978 1 78450 157 0

Can I tell you about Compassion?
Sue Webb
ISBN 978 1 78592 466 8
eISBN 978 1 78450 848 7
Part of the *Can I tell you about…?* series

Giving Children a Voice
A Step-by-Step Guide to Promoting Child-Centred Practice
Sam Frankel
ISBN 978 1 78592 278 7
eISBN 978 1 78450 578 3

Essential Listening Skills for Busy School Staff
What to Say When You Don't Know What to Say
Nick Luxmoore
ISBN 978 1 84905 565 9
eISBN 978 1 78450 000 9

Positive Behaviour Management in Primary Schools
An Essential Guide
Liz Williams
ISBN 978 1 78592 361 6
eISBN 978 1 78450 704 6

Forgiveness is Really Strange
Marina Cantacuzino and Masi Noor
Art by Sophie Standing
ISBN 978 1 78592 124 7
eISBN 978 0 85701 279 1
Part of the *…is Really Strange* series

HOW TO BE A PEACEFUL SCHOOL

PRACTICAL IDEAS, STORIES AND INSPIRATION

Edited by **Anna Lubelska**

Jessica Kingsley *Publishers*
London and Philadelphia

Carl Sandburg quote on page 159 reprinted by arrangement with John Steichen, Paula Steichen Polega and The Barbara Hogenson Agency, Inc.

First published in 2018
by Jessica Kingsley Publishers
73 Collier Street
London N1 9BE, UK
and
400 Market Street, Suite 400
Philadelphia, PA 19106, USA

www.jkp.com

Library of Congress Cataloging in Publication Data
A CIP catalog record for this book is available from the Library of Congress

British Library Cataloguing in Publication Data
A CIP catalogue record for this book is available from the British Library

ISBN 978 1 78592 156 8
eISBN 978 1 78450 424 3

Printed and bound in Great Britain

MIX
Paper from
responsible sources
FSC
www.fsc.org   FSC® C013056

Contents

Introduction 7
Anna Lubelska

1. Peaceful Values 19
    Sue Webb

2. Developing Inner Peace 33
    Pali Nahal

3. Peaceful PSHCE 43
    David Holmes

4. Peaceful Relationships in Primary Schools 59
    Jackie Zammit

5. Peaceful Relationships in Our Secondary School 79
    Helen Floyd

6. A Peaceful Classroom: Creating Space and
    Using Philosophy for Children 95
    Christine Easom

7. The Importance of School Grounds. 115
    Felicity Robinson

8. Peaceful Playtimes 133
    Thérèse Hoyle

9. Our Peaceful School Community 147
    Wendy Phillips

10. Our Peaceful Primary School 159
  Laura Roberts

11. Our Peaceful Secondary School 175
  Cardinal Newman Catholic School Coventry

12. Our Peaceful Special School 185
  Moira Thompson

13. Peace Education for a Better World 199
  Isabel Cartwright

  Concluding Thoughts 215
  Anna Lubelska

  Index 219

INTRODUCTION

Anna Lubelska

Peace in our time

Peace is flowing through our schools, in the classrooms, playgrounds and corridors, fuelled by the energy of passionate pioneers like those who have written about their experiences for this book. Our aim in writing this book is to inspire and motivate you to explore the ways in which you can bring more peace into your lives and your schools.

But first, let us look at this word 'peace' – what do we mean by it? We are talking about something called positive peace,[1] which has been described as creating the best environment for human potential to flourish. It is about working to embed attitudes and values such as respect, fairness, compassion and harmony in our schools. The Peaceful Schools Movement is about building positive peace within all types of schools and spreading peace into the local communities and throughout the world. The Peaceful Schools Movement is a network of schools, organisations and individuals. It is steered by the Peaceful Schools Strategy Group, chaired by Sara Hagel, Director of Peacemakers. We have developed a simple, four-level concept of a peaceful school as a place that grows and sustains peaceful individuals, peaceful relationships, a peaceful school community and peace work in the world. We have promoted this through conferences, support materials and an award scheme, as described later in this introduction.

---

1   Cremin, H. and Bevington, T. (2017) *Positive Peace in Schools*. Oxford: Routledge.

Taking a radical look

We believe that the time has come to take a radical look at the education we need for the twenty-first century. The current over-stressed, over-politicised education system produces stressed teachers and pupils. It does not have to be like this. Schools can be peaceful places where teachers and pupils feel supported and valued and able to spend their time cooperating creatively and learning together. We urge school leaders to take a fresh look at their schools from a new standpoint – to look at how they can make education more holistic and inclusive of spirituality as well as practical and person-centred.

Let us work together

Let us work together to explore how we can create peaceful school communities in which each individual is nurtured and valued. This book shows how this can be done. This book is primarily for anyone involved with schools – school leaders, teachers and other staff as well as parents, governors, pupils and students. In terms of the curriculum, it has particular relevance to: Spiritual, Moral, Social and Cultural (SMSC), Personal, Social, Health, Citizenship and Economic (PSHCE), Religious Education (RE), Inclusion and British Values.

Our chapter authors write about the benefits of working for peace through schools and give practical examples and ideas to make it possible for all schools to become peaceful schools. Even though some of the chapters focus on one type of school, we believe that every chapter has something of relevance to primary, secondary and special schools.

My journey to peaceful schools

My motivation to work for peace has its roots in my childhood. My parents were Holocaust survivors and my life was impacted by the dreadful events of the Second World War. I have a passion to work with people for a better world. My working life started in youth and community work and adult education, then, in the 1990s, I worked at the National Children's Bureau on the rights and well-being of children. Then, in the optimistic and exciting days of 'Every Child Matters',[2]

---

2   Every Child Matters (ECM) was a UK Government initiative for England and Wales, which was launched in 2003, at least partly in response to the death of Victoria Climbié.

I was a Children's Fund Programme Manager and had to set up early intervention services for children through schools and in the community. There was even a time when I was Head of Education at the Association for London Government, and I was involved in the very exciting London Challenge initiative, which was all about improving schools in London.

During the many years of my working life, I developed the conviction that we need schools and services to be more valuing of children and more peace-promoting. In 2007, I set up Spiritual England, a charitable association, with the aim of helping people to lead more peaceful lives and this gave birth to the Peaceful Schools Movement. That is how I came to be called the founder and coordinator of the Peaceful Schools Movement! There are very many people doing great peace work in schools around the UK. My contribution has been to develop the concept of a 'peaceful school' as having four, interconnected levels of peace. I also started calling what we were doing a 'movement' as a way of linking us together, under one banner, so that we could hopefully achieve a collective momentum for change.

Fundamental questions

For me, the questions about the kind of education we need in the future go deeper than current education debates and political arguments about the types of school we should have or the content of the national curriculum. I am interested in more fundamental questions:

- What is a child? Or, to put it more sociologically, what is our social construct of a child? Did you know that in some cultures, a baby is welcomed as a soul coming back to earth with a message for us! How beautiful! In England, we have historically tended to see the child as a young savage in need of discipline and training, and/or an empty vessel in need of filling up with the knowledge of its elders or a citizen-in-waiting that needs to be taught to be a good adult. In so much as I see a child as a spiritual being in a human body, I want children to be respected, listened to and empowered, while also being guided and helped to acquire the skills and abilities to be peacemakers and effective learners.

- What kind of people do we need? I believe that the world needs open-minded, open-hearted, resolute, resilient and highly skilled peacebuilders who can bring that quality and those skills into all their relationships and jobs.

- What are schools for? They used to be for preparing boys to go into the church or the army. Then for producing compliant workers for factories, then administrative cogs for the British Empire, and now it seems that society wants us all to be insatiable consumers! In the twenty-first century, schools should be communities in which pupils and staff can flourish and enjoy learning. They can be workshops of peace, producing peacebuilders with the skills to foster peaceful relationships in their homes and the world.

- What kind of society and world are we working towards? My vision is of a society where we take care of ourselves, others and the Earth and where the inevitable conflicts that occur are resolved through peaceful means. A society where we seek to love ourselves, our neighbours and our enemies.

- Can we work for peace while being prepared to defend our country and helping to keep peace in the world? Yes, we can and we already do. People around the world are using evidence-based effective ways of countering violence with nonviolence, as described by peace activist Scilla Elworthy (2012).[3]

The good news is that there are positive signs of the dawning of a more peaceful age. There is a global desire for change that is encapsulated in the words of the universally acclaimed and much loved spiritual leader, Tenzin Gyatso, His Holiness the 14th Dalai Lama:

There is a great and growing desire for change in the world. Change that ushers in a renewed commitment to ethical and spiritual values, that resolves conflicts peaceably, employing dialogue and

---

3   www.ted.com/talks/scilla_elworthy_fighting_with_non_violence. TEDx talk in Exeter. Accessed 21 November 2017.

non-violence, that upholds human rights and human dignity as well as human responsibility. (2010)[4]

Changing education

Education has certainly changed for the better in my lifetime. When my husband was growing up in a village in Somerset in the fifties, he wasn't allowed to touch the vicar's daughter's desk! You were expected to know your place in society and stick to it. In the seventies, I remember being shocked by the low expectations of the headteacher who showed me round her primary school on the Manor estate in Sheffield where I was the neighbourhood community worker. I was astonished by how she could assert so categorically that: 'None of our children will be going to university.' That is just how it was.

Thankfully, attitudes and expectations have improved, and education has progressed and is more enlightened these days; it is evolving all the time. For example, schools that started out teaching Latin grammar to boys in sterile classrooms now concern themselves with emotional literacy and with creating an attractive learning environment! Schools that once beat and belittled children now pride themselves on having introduced mindfulness sessions for their students. Who could have predicted that? Miracles do happen, but there is more work to be done!

Background to the Peaceful Schools Movement

In 2012, we organised a national conference called 'Peaceful Primary Schools' to launch the Peaceful Schools Movement. We did this in partnership with Quaker Life and the University of Winchester. It was hosted at Friends House in London. As a consequence of the success of the first conference, we set up a Peaceful Schools Strategy Group to build on the energy and enthusiasm for the concept of peaceful schools and to keep the work going beyond the conference. We have since organised two more peaceful schools conferences in partnership with Peacemakers in 2013 and 2016. In 2013, our 'Creating Your Peaceful School' conference was held in Birmingham, where Peacemakers

---

4   www.dalailama.com/messages/world-peace/human-rights-democracy-and-freedom. Accessed 21 November 2017.

are based. A Peaceful Schools film was made at that conference. It can be viewed on our Peaceful Schools website[5] and on YouTube. In 2014, we developed our Peaceful Schools Awards Scheme and set this in motion. Then, in 2016, we held our 'Learning Through Peace Conference' at Friends House in London and we were thrilled to have contributions from some of our Peaceful Schools award winners!

Over recent years, we have been consulting with pupils in primary and secondary schools to get their ideas and thoughts about peace in schools, and we have been working with leaders in the field to produce a range of guidance for people wanting to make their schools peaceful. These are all available as free downloads on our Peaceful Schools website.

The benefits of peaceful schools

In the chapters of this book, our pioneers write about the benefits to children and staff of creating a peaceful environment and of learning the skills to build relationships and deal with conflict in a non-violent way. We have also been excited to see that some schools have improved their Ofsted ratings after going down the Peaceful Schools route. We believe that the benefits for society will be a reduction in bullying, domestic violence and other forms of violent conflict and an improvement in relationships and human flourishing.

In arguing the case for making schools peaceful places, we need the research community to help provide more evidence of the benefits. So far, one study stands out. A research study was set up in 2011, overseen by Professor Peter Fonagy at University College London and his collaborators in Houston, Texas, when trials of an in-school anti-bullying programme suggested that it may be worthwhile to concentrate efforts on creating a peaceful learning environment rather than entirely on tackling the behaviour of the individual bully.[6] The trial in nine schools in the US Mid-West showed that the programme 'Creating a Peaceful School Learning Environment' (CAPSLE), was effective in reducing aggression and victimisation.

---

5   www.peacefulschools.org.uk.
6   www.ncbi.nlm.nih.gov/pubmed/11329408. Accessed 21 November 2017.

The four levels of peace

As already mentioned, our concept of a peaceful school has four, interconnected levels:

Level One: Peace at the individual level (pupils and staff)

Level Two: Peace at the relational level (pair, group or classroom)

Level Three: Peace at a community level (the whole school)

Level Four: Peace at a global level (around and beyond the school)

It is helpful to consider these in more depth.

Level One: Peace at the individual level

This is the foundation level for creating a peaceful school because the well-being of individuals in a school affects everyone else. Pupils have told us that they feel stressed when their teachers are stressed. There are too many stories of teachers being bullied, as well as pupils being bullied, stressed and suffering mental health problems. Our aim is to help pupils and teachers develop their sense of self-worth, their resilience and their ability to feel peaceful. We believe that it is vital that schools put in measures to help pupils and teachers go from stress to calmness. Schools can address this through the experiences and activities that they make available within the school. Some of this is about the everyday experience of being at school. Pupils need to feel that they are being listened to and valued, they need to have quiet times, times of silence, opportunities for contemplation and reflection, as well as being taught mindfulness or meditation and then enabled to practise this on a regular basis. Pupils also need opportunities to be involved in music as well as taking part in activities like yoga, dance and sport. They also need to have good quality food and rest. From our sessions of talking with pupils, we know that many of them are tired and hungry during the day, which has a detrimental impact on their well-being and ability to learn. There is more about this in Chapter 2.

Level Two: Peace at the relational level

This level is about the interaction between individuals within the school – in pairs, groups or in classes. There are many activities and schemes that schools can 'pick and mix' from to suit their particular needs and interests. These activities can be undertaken in many places in the curriculum, not just in PSHCE and RE lessons. Most notably, peace education and peer mediation schemes can make a significant difference to the quality of relationships within a school. Relationship building and mending is covered in all the chapters but most of all in Chapters 3, 4, 5, 6 and 9.

Level Three: Peace at a community level

As we know, the ethos, atmosphere and culture of a school are almost instantly felt when you enter a school, and they influence how everyone within the school behaves. A proven approach to creating a peaceful whole school ethos, is the Values-based Education (VbE) approach (see Chapter 1).

The physical environment of the school, both indoors and outdoors, is important to how people feel and behave at school (see Chapters 7 and 8). The Woodheys Primary School in Sale, Cheshire, is a pioneering example of a peaceful school with wonderful schools grounds. This school was the first in the UK to achieve Beacon Peaceful Schools status (see Chapter 10). Peaceful rooms within schools can be created to supplement the peace of the school library. Such rooms can be used for therapeutic help for children as well as places where children and the adults working in the school can escape from the noise and bustle of the school day. An organisation that is leading the way in this is 'A Quiet Place Ltd' (see Chapter 12).

Level Four: Peace at a global level

This level is about the school and its relationship with the community in which it is located and also the global networks that every school is now part of. Thanks to the internet, we are all actually or potentially connected. An aspect of this, which schools can consider and work on, is how children behave in their families. So, for example, enabling children to practice mindfulness and peer massage within the schools can have 'spill-over' benefits for the families. Another aspect would be inviting parents and others to come into the school, either individually or in larger numbers, so that they can participate in activities, such as the creation of a peaceful garden, and in special events that build relationships between parents of different backgrounds, cultures and religions. Schools can enable students to go out into the community as peace workers or peace ambassadors. An example of students acting this way was demonstrated when secondary school students challenged arms traders at a trade fair in London (see Chapter 13).

Our Peaceful Schools awards scheme

Thanks in large part to the work of David Holmes, a member of the Peaceful Schools Strategy Group, we developed a pilot Peaceful Schools Awards Scheme with three different award categories: the Peacemaker Award, the Peaceful Project Award and the Beacon Peaceful School Award. You might be interested to learn a bit more about these.

The Peacemaker Award is open to children, young people and adults of all ages because no one is too young or too old to be an ambassador of peace! Being a 'peacemaker' is not about a personal journey of peace – although that will be an important part of why they have made the contribution that is being celebrated. It is given to acknowledge and recognise those individuals who have made a significant personal contribution to promoting any or all of the following: the personal peace of others, peaceful relationships, peaceful school communities and a peaceful world.

The Peaceful Project Award is applicable to three types of projects. It can be a peace-focused project with a specific timescale that has been undertaken and completed, for example when a school works on something specific with a partner organisation for a limited number of weeks. Second, it can be a peace-focused project that has been put in place and is then ongoing, like the creation of a peace garden or a quiet indoor area. Third, the 'project' can be changes to school practice, policies and organisation that have been put in place with the specific aim of promoting and enhancing peace such as changing the school's 'behaviour' policy to a 'relationships' policy and amending the pupil rewards scheme to ensure that it includes pupils' contribution to peace within the school.

The Beacon Peaceful School Award is all about the individual school. It is important that it reflects the school as a community and how the journey of peace has impacted on those involved. This award is not about ticking boxes to show what has been done. It is about sharing why peace is important to the school and how the school's commitment to it has impacted on lives, ethos, culture, practices and purpose. This award is given for a school's achievements in all four of the peaceful school levels of individual peace, peaceful relationships, peaceful communities and peace work in the world.

The chapters in this book

I am extremely grateful to everyone who has contributed to this book. Between them, our chapter authors cover the four levels of peace that we have identified as being essential to peaceful schools work: inner peace, peaceful relationships, peaceful community and peace in the world. The four levels of peace interact with one another and the chapters cover all levels in one way or another, although they might have a specific focus on one of the levels. Each chapter gives you practical information and ideas about how a school can be made to be a place of peaceful interactions and a generator of peace that can 'flood out'[7] into the world.

Chapter 1 is by Sue Webb, former Headteacher of a primary school in Buckinghamshire. Her school achieved a Beacon Peaceful School Award. Sue writes about the way in which the school implemented Values-based Education and what a difference it made to the pupils and the school. In Chapter 2, Pali Nahal, former Headteacher of a primary school in the West Midlands, shares key aspects of her Beacon Peaceful School and shows how being a peaceful school has helped them to achieve being in the top 10 per cent for progress based on their results, and also how it has helped create a highly effective school environment where the children are at the heart of everything they do.

Chapter 3 is by David Holmes, a member of the Peaceful Schools Strategy Group and a retired primary school Headteacher, a Healthy Schools Advisor in Derbyshire and author of several of our Peaceful

---

7   This phrase was coined by a primary school pupil from one of the Beacon Peaceful Schools.

Schools publications and guidance booklets available as free downloads on the Peaceful Schools website. David takes a look at what schools are required to deliver in terms of the national curriculum for primary schools and sets that in the context of what it can mean to be a peaceful school. He explores what is meant by 'peace' before going on to look in more detail about how we can approach PSHCE from a peaceful perspective.

In Chapter 4, Jackie Zammit, trainer with Peacemakers, a dynamic charity based in the West Midlands, shares some of the foundations for peace on which their work is based and then describes some of the practical approaches that they use in schools for whole class, child and adult learning. In Chapter 5, Helen Floyd, School Chaplain at Oaklands Catholic School and Sixth Form College in Hampshire, writes about her very successful reconciliation work. Helen is a Peacemaker Award winner. She describes the 'reconciliation meeting' process that she has developed in detail and includes examples of feedback from students who have experienced the process and from staff who have referred them to the process.

In Chapter 6, Christine Easom, a former Head of the religious education department in a secondary school in Staffordshire, writes about her experiences of creating a peaceful classroom and exploring peace with primary and secondary school pupils using Philosophy for Children (P4C). Then, in Chapter 7, Felicity Robinson, a teacher and landscape architect, looks at why and how learning, play and recreation outside in the grounds is important and valued in many schools. Felicity also offers you an audit checklist of points to consider when looking at your own school grounds. Following on from that, in Chapter 8, Thérèse Hoyle, shares her knowledge and experience of running and developing Positive Playtime and Lunchtime Training Programmes in schools.

In Chapter 9, Wendy Phillips, Learning Mentor at St Andrew's RC Primary in Lambeth, another Beacon Primary School, writes about the school's vibrant and loving peace work with pupils, families and the community. Then, in Chapter 10, Laura Roberts, who was Headteacher of the first ever Beacon Peaceful School, Woodheys Primary in Sale, Cheshire, writes about her journey of creating a peaceful school with a strong interfaith element, using the Peace Mala scheme. This is followed in Chapter 11 by Cardinal Newman Secondary School in Coventry, the first ever Beacon Peaceful Secondary School. They write about the journey the school has been on, and continues to be on, as a Beacon Peaceful School.

The author of Chapter 12 is Moira Thompson, the Headteacher of Hawthorns Community School in the Manchester area. It is a special school for pupils with complex needs. Moira writes about their work to bring peace into the lives of their children with support from their partner organization – A Quiet Place Ltd.

Finally, in Chapter 13, Isabel Cartwright, a member of the Peaceful Schools Strategy Group and the Peace Education Programme Manager for Quakers in Britain, explores the concept of peace education and her team's work in schools, referring to a project called 'Fly Kites Not Drones'. Isabel also describes a 'Peace Week' carried out in two London primary schools. The chapter concludes by looking at the challenges of the society in which we live, and how and where we should start tackling these challenges.

CHAPTER 1

PEACEFUL VALUES

Sue Webb

Introduction

In my view, our rapidly changing world certainly needs changing for the better in so many ways. Educating children about peace within themselves first will create more peaceful individuals, more peaceful societies and, as an ideal outcome, a more peaceful world. This work is happening in some of our schools and it is a joy to see. It is obvious to me that by underpinning the culture and curriculum in our schools with values such as peace, respect, equality and compassion, we will cultivate peaceful hearts and minds in our future generations.

It is funny how life turns out. I did not plan to be a teacher but it became my dream job. Becoming a headteacher also was not part of my plan, but somehow that happened, too. It was a joy and a privilege to lead a school community that was so open to the great, positive changes that we drove through together during my time as headteacher of The Downley School, a large primary school in High Wycombe, Buckinghamshire. In July 2014, I was delighted that our school was awarded Beacon Peaceful School status.

When I arrived at the school in the autumn of 2010, I quickly realised that there was a huge amount of work that needed to be done in almost all aspects of school life. I asked a highly esteemed colleague, Roy Blatchford, then Director of the National Education Trust, to visit the school and benchmark it for me. Among the many suggestions for improvement, his parting words stayed with me forever: 'You've got a sleeping giant here, Sue. You need to wake him up!' There was so much untapped potential in the school! We could not do everything at once, but we set about making rapid and positive changes, starting with building a culture of openness, honesty and trust, where people felt valued. This was the start of everyone's individual journeys to becoming their best selves.

Over the next two years, many changes were made as we worked extremely hard to wake the sleeping giant and to provide our children with a genuinely outstanding education. After a year, the giant was stirring. After two years, he was awake but still a bit dozy. And that is when I met Dr Neil Hawkes, a renowned educationalist, a former headteacher and the founder of Values-based Education (VbE). This meeting was to change my life and the life of the school community. I now spend much of my time with Neil and VbE, working passionately to encourage and support as many schools as possible on their unique values journeys. We help schools to become enlightened as to how staff and pupils have a much better chance of fulfilling their wonderful potential when a culture of values authentically permeates the school. VbE creates environments where the importance of well-being to learning and good mental health is highly regarded and central to everything, and people flourish in such places!

What is 'Values-based Education'?

Values-based Education was pioneered by a headteacher in a large Oxfordshire school in the early nineties. The headteacher was Neil Hawkes and the school was West Kidlington Primary School. Having been a teacher for many years, Neil had formed theories about the impact of underpinning a school culture and curriculum explicitly with values-based language and behaviours. Neil simultaneously embarked on a DPhil at Oxford University as he introduced what we now know as Values-based Education and saw what he had theorised lived out in his school. The impact was astounding as a whole school community embedded a set of shared values. The pupils acquired high levels of personal and social competences that led to deep, authentic relationships and improved academic learning behaviours and outcomes. This was the beginning of a movement that is now worldwide and shows school communities a way of embedding a culture through which everyone is encouraged to flourish and achieve:

> It's a movement which provides our students with a dynamic compass at school and throughout the rest of their lives, strengthening their

resilience and well-being. It nurtures the development of good character, deep thinking and altruistic behaviour. The outcome of VbE is the positive transformation of individuals and institutions – exactly what our world needs. (Hawkes)[1]

A whole school approach

I knew as soon as I met Neil and heard about VbE that that was what our school needed! The giant needed a heart transplant so that he could wake up properly and thrive. When my leadership team heard about VbE, they agreed and Neil visited our school for the first time so as to talk to us more about the possibility of whole school change. It was essential that the entire school community were on board with this initiative; they had seen so many changes in the previous two years, many of which had 'come from the top' and involved a great deal of hard work. I was determined that this was not going to be something that was going to be 'done to them'. This had to be something that they wanted, a shared vision and something about which everyone could feel a sense of ownership.

I organised a whole school INSET day for the start of the new academic year. In September 2012, the entire staff of the school (as well as several governors) enjoyed a brilliant day with Neil. He reinforced the message that every member of staff was as valued as anyone else and encouraged everyone to contribute their unique experiences and personal hopes for the school. Many of the non-teaching members of staff were apprehensive before the day, wondering why they had to attend a training day that was traditionally seen as being for teaching staff only. By the end of the day, everyone was excited, refreshed and motivated to bring VbE to the school as soon as possible.

We started the process. There is a template that VbE suggests to follow as a school works towards embedding a values-based culture and ethos. This 'values template' works for all schools: primary, secondary, academies, multi-academy trusts, free, independent and international because it can be adapted to each school's context and community. All elements of the template are essential to the successful implementation of VbE. The first one being that the whole school community chooses the values that are important and relevant to them.

---

1   Speaking at 'Values-based Education' conference in Enfield in 2016.

So, at Downley, each member of staff had chosen values that they thought were important to the school. Pupils had also been asked and so had governors. We decided to invite the parents and other members of the local community to a meeting with Neil Hawkes in order for them to hear from the founder of VbE and contribute their thoughts on which values should be included. By doing this, we hoped that they would feel completely engaged with the process that was to make the school a very special place for their children to attend.

Altogether, we ended up with a list of between 40 and 50 values. We were planning to explore one value a month over a period of two academic years, so we needed 22. I created a simple electronic survey that we sent to all stakeholders, asking them to choose their 'Top 10'. A few days later, we had our 22 core school values! They included values such as respect, compassion, honesty, determination, equality, cooperation and positivity.

Happily, one of the values that was in our list was 'peace'. It was wonderful to focus on the value of peace for a month and it had a positive impact. However, a much more profound change happened as we explored each value over the period of two years; the school transformed into a genuinely 'Peaceful School' through the culture that we built and the ethos of values that we embedded into the very core of everything that we did.

Developing each of the aspects of the VbE 'template' through exploring a new value each month meant that our school was becoming a place where everyone started to 'live the values'. When people are living and showing values such as respect, tolerance, compassion and courage, then after a relatively short time you have a much more peaceful community. Imagine if all schools did this! Month by month, we focused on the transformational elements of VbE and the giant's new heart started to beat strongly.

The transformational elements of VbE

Role modelling

It was crucial that everyone in the school, without exception, took on the responsibility of being a model of the kind of human beings that we wanted our children to become. As you might imagine, this took many of us on our own internal journeys of self-awareness! It was a joy to see people thinking about how they showed up to the outside world, both to the children and to each other. For some staff, it was their natural way of being. For others, it was hard to accept this responsibility. Suddenly, they had to really take on board that they must show our young people the kind of adults we all wanted them to grow up to be. Knowing it and showing it were quite different things for some people. When I left the school, one member of staff who had struggled with negativity and lack of self-confidence had me in tears as she courageously opened up about her personal life to me and explained the causes of her behaviour. Her point in doing this was to explain to me the changes that had happened to her over the time we had been a values-based school and to thank me for bringing changes to the school that had helped her to face her personal challenges and grow as a person.

In a school where everyone wants the very best for the children, it follows that they want the very best for each other. Warm, supportive relationships developed as staff gently, but uncompromisingly, supported each other in becoming the change they wanted to see in the school. It was also a joy to see how children realised that they could explicitly become role models for each other.

Inner curriculum

This is a concept coined by Neil and his wife Jane, who is a psychotherapist. With the latest developments in neuroscience, we can recognise that the development of different parts of the brain is essential to help us to be aware and in control of our internal world of thoughts, feelings and emotions. This enables us to respond appropriately to others without hurting them or damaging our own sense of self. This is quite a revelation to many in education, and schools are gradually beginning to recognise the importance of training their staff in such concepts as attachment, awareness and emotion coaching, so that we can relate to how children are thinking and feeling in terms of what is happening in the brain. This new knowledge and these skills help us to support children in the best possible way. Leaders in this field include Dr Dan Siegel in the USA and Dr Janet Rose at Bath Spa University (Emotional Coaching UK) (see Further Reading and Organisations and Websites). It is a huge field of work, but for staff in the classroom, the question is: 'How can we develop the areas of the brain needed for such emotional and social well-being?' One of the ways is the third element of VbE.

Reflection

This is about 'stilling the mind' or giving the brain time to 'be quiet'. It is also about breathing and relaxing. Realising the benefits of such activity, some schools have started a formal programme of mindfulness. The 'Mindfulness in Schools Project' website lists its own research studies and links to research done by other organisations. In all schools, however, ensuring that there is a time for silent reflection or for a quiet visualisation every day can have a profound effect on children's learning. We all know that a lot of time is wasted in schools after breaktimes when pupils have had (small or large) conflicts with each other. Playgrounds are often not the most peaceful places! If children are in a daily routine of coming into the classroom, finding their own space and spending time on an activity of reflection, almost all tension is dissolved. Emotions are calmed, bodies relax and neural pathways are developed. The more this practice is embedded, the more calm and peaceful classrooms become. That is not to say that serious conflicts should not be given the appropriate attention. However, as a culture of values becomes embedded, a school becomes a place where children recognise the consequences of their actions on others and conflict in general becomes a rarity.

At Downley, it was clear that over a period of time, more children were developing an increasingly internal framework to regulate their behaviours. With growing emotional literacy and ethical vocabulary, role models and practice of reflective activities, we needed to use far less external strategies such as rewards and sanctions. We encouraged and noticed the development of much more authentic behaviours and celebrated this change in our school.

Atmosphere

You will know a 'values-based' school as soon as you walk into it – if not before. Many VbE schools work with artistic partners to create a sculpture of some kind to welcome visitors to the school and to celebrate values. As you approach The Downley School, for example, you will see a huge, beautiful metallic tree. A grant from three separate organisations funded the most wonderful partners, Pete Rogers and Alex Hallowes of Xceptional Designs, who worked with every child and many members of staff in the school. The outcome was a child-led design in which the school's values were encapsulated. Each beautiful aluminium leaf was created by a group of children and represents a value.

Inside a values-based school, you are greeted with warmth and respect by all staff and pupils. You feel the ethos as you explore the stimulating values-based environment. You notice the quality of the displays, the helpful signage, the cleanliness, the organisation and management of resources, the calm working atmosphere, the friendly and courteous behaviour of adults and children. Perhaps most of all, you notice the authentically respectful behaviour of all staff and pupils and how this leads to the fostering of deep, safe and peaceful relationships. Of course, this culture has a hugely positive impact on teaching and learning, thus allowing for a deeper development of the next element.

Curriculum

Values are taught explicitly in some Personal, Social, Health and Citizenship Education (PSHCE) lessons, but much more exploration and experiential learning occurs in other lessons throughout the whole curriculum. I have had the privilege to watch many lessons in values-based schools now, and I notice how the most effective lessons are always underpinned by values language. For example, teachers in Maths lessons often refer to values in order to encourage a growth mindset: 'I know you can work your way through this challenge with perseverance and determination' or 'A superb effort! You all showed excellent teamwork skills in working together to solve this maths problem.' Philosophy for Children (P4C) lessons and techniques are a wonderful way to encourage deeper exploration of values through creative, collaborative and caring thinking. In my experience, teachers who naturally use values-associated language create superb learning environments, where pupils learn to be teachers, too, and become role models of values. In visiting many values-based schools, I notice that the relationship between staff and pupils is *the* most important factor in the nurturing and growing of values role models. I have seen wonderful nursery-aged role models, superb sixth formers leading the way, and all ages in between. One of my strongest memories is of some secondary-aged pupils at a special setting – Rowdeford School. The relationships between the amazingly dedicated and values-driven staff and their students was humbling. I was absolutely awestruck by how pupils with severe learning difficulties, and all the associated challenges, demonstrated their school values (respect, resilience, caring, cooperation, responsibility and happiness) so deeply and authentically.

Leadership

It is great leadership that initially drives a values-based culture in a school. In my experience, great 'values-leaders' come in many guises but have much in common. They are visionary and brave. They recognise what is right for their school and they are uncompromising in their efforts to improve the organisation for the whole community. They are authentic in their desire for their staff and children to experience the very best that education has to offer. They bring a positive energy to the organisation and show up with the confidence and capability to inspire others and support them all the way with compassion and generosity of time and talents. Although appearing to 'talk the soft stuff', people quickly realise that values-leaders are anything but soft. They function at a very high level, thinking strategically and creatively towards the optimum outcomes in an educational world full of deep complexity and unrelenting challenge. This quality of leadership builds the foundations of a values-based school, but the organisation only grows and flourishes when other leaders emerge and take responsibility for recognising and driving a values agenda in their roles.

I have found that the wonderful thing about working in a values-based school is that everyone can become a leader and have their work celebrated. Playground supervisors, support staff, teachers, site staff, managers, office staff, governors and especially the children, can all be seen as leaders in a school. One awesome member of staff in my school, Tony, was a lunchtime supervisor and also a cleaner. He was *the* most values-based human being! He was a model of compassion, care, courage, integrity, respect and just about every other value you can think of. His language was naturally values-based and he thrived in an environment where he was recognised as a role model. It was a joy to watch him grow in confidence and regard himself as a leader of values (although he would never have said that himself).

Two Year 6 pupils, Hannah and Hazel, were also wonderful values-leaders. They initiated a Values Council in our school, recruited pupils to it, held fortnightly meetings and drove initiatives right the way through the school. When they went on to secondary school, they made sure to leave the Values Council with two new fully trained-up leaders to carry on their great work. I hear that their secondary school has learned a great deal from these two amazing leaders as well. As more and more adults and children in the school community take personal responsibility for their thoughts, behaviour and actions, we see the development of the final, and probably most impactful, element of VbE.

Ethical vocabulary

A critical outcome of VbE is greater self-awareness and emotional empathy, leading to what can be described as ethical intelligence. Values words create a universal narrative so that people can talk about important issues. After embarking on the values journey for a few months, I slowly became aware of a significant shift in the language being used by everyone around me. It is true that everyone was involved in choosing the school's values – but it is when they start to become 'lived' that the shift happens. In our school, the first few values that we explored were love, compassion, respect, kindness, responsibility, friendship and peace. It is important to recognise that these words are rooted in all the major world religions and non-religions, too. They are universal positive human values. As I visit many values-based schools, I see some differences in values that have been chosen, but I see vast commonality in how the values are interpreted and lived in everyday life.

The 'shift' happens when the language changes. When language changes, behaviour changes. The root of this change is the development of ethical intelligence at an individual level, which permeates the school and starts to create a community of human beings who understand themselves at a deeper level, and this growing self-awareness means that they understand each other at a deeper level. Then something beautiful happens. Relationships become more meaningful. Children and adults start to see the world through one another's eyes. They show genuine respect, empathy, tolerance and compassion towards one another. Their behaviour is driven by positive values rather than by conforming out of fear of negative responses or punishment. They use their growing emotional and ethical intelligences to make decisions that have more positive outcomes for themselves and others. They are able to communicate using their growing ethical vocabulary, to find words to express how they feel and how they have made others feel. They take responsibility for their own actions and realise the consequences of their actions on others. When people think about these consequences before they actually take the action, you have a population who are making values-based decisions – people who can use values-centric language to create a new narrative and to solve problems in a values-based way. Imagine if this was to happen throughout the world!

VbE in practice

To get a feel of a month in the life of a values-based school, let's reflect on the value of 'peace'. We chose to focus on this value in the month of September, to coincide with the United Nation's annual International Day of Peace on 21 September. I have been an avid follower of the work of the founder of Peace One Day, Jeremy Gilley, who worked so hard to create this day of peace and to get the United Nations to adopt it. For many years, now and every year, I have done my best to share information about this special day. A few people have been interested. Now, it has become a major event for our school community, and suddenly hundreds more people are aware of the importance of peace and how they could make their individual contribution to a more peaceful world. September started with a whole school Values Assembly that I created and delivered. As our new value was revealed, the children and staff became intrigued and enthusiastic about the month ahead.

All values assemblies launch the new value, whilst reminding everyone of the values we have already learned about and now have in our 'values toolkits' in our hearts and minds. So, we took a moment of quietness to reflect on the values of 'love', 'compassion', 'respect', 'kindness', 'responsibility' and 'friendship' and how these had *changed our thinking and behaviour*. When a value is explained as something that changes your thinking and behaviour, children understand the concept very quickly. They are able to reflect on a value and talk articulately about how their thinking and behaviour has changed as a result of their learning and living a particular value. The assembly was shared with parents so they could talk about the value of 'peace' with their children at home. It aimed to raise awareness of how we live our lives in alignment with this value, how important it is to us and how we can help to create a more peaceful world. The main message from the assembly was that peace starts in your own heart, and by being peaceful in our own behaviour, we can start to affect change in the environment around us. This was to be strongly reinforced throughout the month by all staff in school and hopefully by parents, too. As the month went on, children became wonderful role models of this message.

Anyone visiting the school was immediately aware of our values focus, such was the atmosphere of peace. It was explicit through displays in the foyer and every classroom and through lessons being underpinned with this value. It was implicit in staff and children recognising peaceful behaviours in each other and expressing their appreciation of this with positive praise to each other. Moments of stillness became moments to focus on the value of peace and reflect on how we each were helping to make our own worlds of home, school and community more peaceful places. We learned much more about the work of Peace One Day through the month and worked towards celebrating International Day of Peace on 21 September. Each class researched the impact of this day on people of the world and created their own piece of work to share with the rest of the school in an assembly at the end of the month. As 21 September was a Saturday, we celebrated off-timetable on the Friday to work specifically on peaceful projects. We also sent out information for parents to be able to tune into the Peace One Day live broadcast on the Saturday. Subsequently, the children presented their peace work to each other in assembly the week after International Peace Day. Many talked about feeling part of a more peaceful world and also of being able to play their part in creating a more peaceful world.

When we moved on to explore the new value of 'equality' in October, we did not forget about 'peace'. We took it deeper, built on what we had learned and explored the connections between these and the other values we had learned about. Over the following months, each individual's understanding of the concept of peace became more and more rooted in their lives.

Concluding thoughts

I feel privileged to have met Dr Neil Hawkes and to have been in the position to have encouraged staff, pupils, parents and governors to work together to become a values-based school community. In July of 2014, my school was recognised as a 'Beacon Peaceful School', which was an honour we were delighted to receive.

As the initiative progressed, the giant's heart grew stronger and stronger. He not only woke up but jumped up and started to dance with joy! And we all danced with him, our hearts and minds full of values and our school full of well-being, peace and happiness!

Hope for the future

VbE gives me hope for the future. The pace of change in the world is accelerating at an unprecedented rate and whilst this brings some positive changes, many people I talk to, both inside and outside of the educational sphere, are concerned about the impact of such rapid changes, especially on our young people. Personally, at times I am terrified for the future of our world. As we live through increasingly rapid changes in technology, globalisation and nature (some good, many bad), we need strong, authentic leaders of the world who are driven by positive human values and who can work to solve the global problems facing us. We need leaders who are empathetic, courageous, altruistic, compassionate, honest and truly respectful. We need these leaders to work with wisdom and collaboration in order to slow down the rate of change and help us to keep in touch with our human selves; to help us live with self-respect and with respect for each other. These leaders of the future are coming through our schools right now – we are teaching them! My hope for the world is that they are being nurtured and educated to lead values-centric lives and to form relationships based on positive human values and that one day our world will be a truly peaceful place where we are able to trust, follow and support leaders who know what humanity needs to flourish.

What drives me is the vision for every school to be a values-based school in whatever way is best for them. That every person within that school is encouraged to live in alignment with their own values and those shared by the different communities of which they are a part. I wish for parents to choose schools for their children because they want the values they are bringing their children up with to be reinforced and developed as part of their formal education. As educators and parents, let's make sure that we are doing the very best we can to grow every single child to be a positive and passionate global citizen, and a leader in their own right. The outcome of our energy will be leaders of the world who make the best decisions for our shared humanity and for the peaceful world we all desire in our hearts.

Further reading

Hawkes, N. (2013) *From My Heart: Transforming Lives through Values*. Bancyfelin: Independent Thinking Press an imprint of Crown House Publishing.

Siegel, D. (2010) *Mindsight: The New Science of Personal Transformation*. New York: Bantam.

Siegel, D. and Payne-Bryson, T. (2011) *The Whole-Brain Child: 12 Revolutionary Strategies to Nurture Your Child's Developing Mind, Survive Everyday Parenting Struggles and Help Your Family Thrive*. New York: Delacorte Press.

Organisations and websites

www.drdansiegel.com

www.emotioncoachinguk.com

www.mindfulnessinschools.org/research

www.rowdeford.wilts.sch.uk

www.sapere.org.uk

www.thedownleyschool.org

www.valuesbasededucation.com

CHAPTER 2

DEVELOPING INNER PEACE

Pali Nahal

Introduction

As an educator and leader with over ten years of leadership experience, I soon learned how important it is to develop a peaceful ethos through shared values and listening to children's views. In our school, the children drive the ideas and creativity. As a result, we have developed not only a school where they learn but also an environment where they are safe, happy and feel cared for. What is more, they are proud of their school!

Blackheath Primary School (BPS) serves one of England's most deprived wards and is ranked lowest out of 109 areas for both employment and income. There are 500 children on roll, with the majority of children being of white British origin. A quarter of our vulnerable families are supported by the school through parenting programmes and interventions. Pupils' attainment on entry is significantly below the national average for all subjects.

In this chapter, I share key aspects of our Beacon Peaceful School to show how being a peaceful school has helped us to achieve being in the top 10 per cent for progress based on our results and also how it has helped us create a highly effective school environment, where the children are at the heart of everything we do.

Our journey starts

When you close your eyes and think of peace, what do you see? Perhaps it is a cloud, perhaps you see yourself sitting, soaking in the sun on a beach or listening to music or reading your favourite book or magazine. To start our journey of developing inner peace, we asked our children the same question, 'When you close your eyes and think of peace, what do you see?' in order to find out what peace means to them. We were surprised by some of the responses:

> 'Peace is when we trust, not hate.'

> 'Peace is sitting under my bed because it's where I feel safe.'

> 'Peace is having calm, happy feelings and not thinking bad about anything or anyone.'

As a school leader, I had a vision of developing a culture and ethos for becoming a peaceful school. I wanted to create a calm, quiet and relaxed environment giving our whole school community a sense of peace when they are in school, and I am proud to say that we have successfully achieved this! It is music to my ears when we have visitors comment on the relaxed and peaceful ethos we have created.

Our school values

We started our journey by working together as a staff team and creating a set of values that the whole school community could embrace. The biggest difficulty was in coming up with an acronym but, three staff meetings later, we finally came up with RESPECT:

R – RESPONSIBILITY (Everyone's)

E – EMPATHY (Show understanding)

S – SMART (Appearance in everything)

P – POLITENESS (Be polite at all times)

E – EMPOWER (Let me learn/lead for myself)

C – CARE (Show you care about yourself, each other and your environment)

T – TEAM (Together Everyone Achieves More)

So as to ensure that children understood each of the values, we launched a 'value of the week' in a weekly assembly. We put up posters around the school and talked regularly with the children about each value as it was launched so that they could develop an excellent understanding of each of the values and how they could apply these at home and school. Towards the end of the first term after launching the values, we realised that, although the children were excited about the values, the excitement was fading. We knew what our vision was and that we wanted to change the culture in school and so we thought creatively about how to sustain a values-based community.

We asked parents and children to redesign the school logo in line with our seven values of RESPECT. You can see this on our school website.[1] Each colour represents a specific value and each value is represented by a values puppet: Responsible Roger, Empathy Eddie, Smart Sammy, Polite Polly, Empowering Ella, Caring Clive, Team Tahira. The puppets visit classes for a week and go out to the playground to talk to children about the value that they represent. This creative approach raised the profile of our values and it was certainly the talk of the playground for months! Following on from the launch of the puppets, we reviewed our behaviour policy so that children could earn 'values points'. An online system was set up so that these can be recorded by all the adults, and the children are able to collect and save their points. Every week, children are able to exchange their values points for prizes on the school's 'Golden Trolley'. They have the option of spending their points weekly. Some children save their values points for the whole year so that they can save for a bigger prize. Not only has this encouraged children to demonstrate our RESPECT values, but it has also encouraged them to think about the way they spend their earnings.

We have also developed specific behaviour and learning rules that are aligned with our school values. This has ensured a common language about expectations across the school environment.

The creative and innovative implementation of a school values-based education has proven to be highly effective in our school. Everyone in the whole school community is confidently able to name and apply RESPECT within all areas of school life and they have played a huge part in embedding personal values in the hearts and lives of our children. Without the implementation and application of our school values, we would not have created the inner peace that lives within the school ethos.

---

1   www.blackheathprimary.org.uk.

School environment

Creating inner peace in the mind is possible in any environment but creating an environment which children are proud of, and one in which they feel completely safe and can enjoy, gives them the opportunity to influence their wellbeing. Although our school building was only ten years old, it lacked creativity and spark. The light-blue painted blocks throughout the school gave it quite an empty and bare feel. We involved our children in redesigning the corridors and took onboard their suggestions. We started by creating four mini academies:

Explorers Academy – Nursery and Reception

Creators Academy – Year 1 and Year 2

Challengers Academy – Year 3 and Year 4

Innovators Academy – Year 5 and Year 6

The purpose of the restructure to the school's existing 'key stages or phases' was to give the children a real sense of belonging and raise their aspirations. Children leaving the school at the end of Year 6 had gone through the school having been an explorer, creator, challenger and innovator. When the children leave each academy at the end of the year, we have a graduation ceremony, where they are proud to wear the graduation attire of a cap and gown and are presented with an award for their successes during their time in their academy. In line with our academy structure, we designed our corridors with a similar theme to the academy name. All corridor spaces are interactive, creative and innovative in their unique designs:

- Our Explorers Academy has a jungle-themed corridor, in which there are seated areas, interactive displays and activities. Sounds of the rainforest and jungle play continually as well as smells of the jungle! We also have our pet cockatiel 'Columbus', who lives in the jungle and gets many visitors throughout the day.

- Our Creators Academy corridor theme was designed by staff and children. We have four classrooms that are focused around art, music, drama and construction. The children decided that they wanted the area outside the construction classroom to have a Lego and Minecraft theme with creative music playing continually!

- Our Challengers Academy has a climbing wall that the children can use, as well as challenging games that the children can play.

- Our Innovators Academy corridor has been converted to a space station, with innovative artefacts and resources that the children can handle. You can hear sounds from space as you walk through the Innovators Academy.

Having a range of music playing within the different academies helps to immerse you in the environment as you walk through. Music has been a huge part of creating a peaceful school. Regularly during the day, classical music is used in classrooms to create an ambience and an escape for the children's thoughts.

To add to our peaceful environment, we have created our peaceful garden and school forest. This space has allowed us to create a real tranquil, safe space, where children can become immersed in their own thoughts. We have a sensory room for those pupils who would benefit from a multisensory space. For children with special educational needs in particular, a busy mainstream school often lacks the much needed space for these children to develop their own inner peace, and our sensory room allows children to do this.

Social, emotional and mental health

After creating our effective peaceful environment, one of our biggest challenges was to review our curriculum so as to ensure that it was also addressing the social, emotional and mental health (SEMH) of our children. It was also a time to reflect and ensure that opportunities within the curriculum were given to children to develop their SEMH. In line with our curriculum topics, we developed the 'BPS 50' (BPS stands for 'Blackheath Primary School'). These were 50 memorable experiences that the children would take part in by the time they left our school!

Each half-termly topic was linked to a relevant memorable experience. For example, Year 6's topic 'Frozen Kingdom' gives children the opportunity to experience the thrill and excitement of riding with husky dogs. Our 'Beast Creator' topic allows children to handle animals and care for them. Our school hall is converted into Jurassic Park during our Year 1 'Dinosaur Planet' topic and, in Year 4, our children get the opportunity to complete basic first-aid training linked to their topic.

Some of our memorable experiences are linked specifically to developing inner peace. We make a peace tree and we have a prayer tree, where children can write a prayer or express their gratitude. All of these experiences give the children a real excitement about their learning. They are immersed in their learning and fully engaged before they even start their topic. As well as topic-linked experiences, children have the opportunity to learn to ride a bike, have free swimming lessons and complete a kickboxing or boxing qualification. More importantly, our menu of extracurricular activities develops their own confidence and range of skills and raises their own aspirations for the future.

Pupil leadership teams

One of our approaches to developing confidence and real life skills was the introduction of ten pupil leadership teams across the school. These include Digital Leaders, Green Hat Thinkers, School Council and Playground Buddies. The roles are advertised in the summer term and children have to complete an application form to apply. The Committee Leaders, who are staff members, then look through the application forms and invite those children who have been shortlisted to an interview. Children are then formally interviewed and once appointed, a job offer letter is given to them. Once they accept the position, they work collaboratively within their committees to develop an action plan. They attend termly meetings to evaluate the action plan and plan next steps.

The children have a significant role to play in whole school strategic decisions, and I can honestly say that sometimes we have felt quite uncomfortable with their requests. However, we have been proven wrong, as their decisions and requests have always turned out to be successful, despite taking the risk. For example, we asked the children how they would spend the Government-funded sports premium grant. They had ideas of buying an outdoor children's gym and having Didi cars available to children, so that children could take part in fun sports. They were absolutely right and, without their input, I cannot confidently say that the impact would have been so great. The children also decided on the themes of the corridors. Compared to the adults' inputs, their ideas were far more creative, innovative and modern.

This has been proved in our amazing corridor environment space. You can see photos of these on our school website.

Spiritual learning

To enhance our curriculum further and also to create a truly peaceful culture and ethos, we reviewed our spiritual, moral, social and cultural (SMSC) provision. Part of our work in this area was to further develop our spiritual learning and this involved exploring beliefs and experiences; respecting faiths, feelings and values; learning about ourselves, others and the surrounding world; as well as using imagination and creativity, and instilling the skills needed for reflection.

Our spiritual provision is provided through our multicultural experiences, visits to places of worship, having a culture week every year, links with two international schools with live Skype sessions during assemblies and our ten pupil leadership teams. As an accredited 'Edward de Bono Thinking School', imagination and creativity was already part of our teaching philosophy.

We further developed our curriculum topics so that children had the chance to reflect on their learning as well as their experiences. We introduced a weekly yoga session across the school. We also hold a weekly 'Mindfulness Monday' assembly. This was a great way to settle children back into the school ethos after the weekend. Children actively engage in the assembly, and the feedback from the children is that they find it relaxing and often think about the mindfulness stories when they relax at home.

We have also introduced a daily colour therapy session within the school timetable. This takes place for ten minutes straight after lunch and, again, it has been really effective in settling children back into a peaceful environment after a busy lunchtime. Children are protective and proud of their colour therapy books and the coloured pencil packs that we provide for all children. During colour therapy, teachers play a range of classical music.

For individual children who find it difficult to manage their own behaviour, we have a range of strategies to support their spiritual learning so that they can get to know themselves and then identify how best to manage their own outbursts. We start by completing a behaviour support plan with the child, which identifies strategies that they prefer the adults to use with them. This allows the child to control their management of their behaviour so that they start understanding what works for them and they develop their own self-regulation skills. This is followed by a range of strategies, including zone boards, peace bags, chill-out zones, morning journals and a regular chat with a key worker. The strapline that we use with some of our pupils is: 'It's OK to be angry, it's what we do that matters.' This has been highly effective in developing inner peace for children who have behaviourial needs.

'Healthy Minds'

Our provision for social, emotional and mental health is truly innovative and highly supportive of addressing the needs of our children. 'Healthy Minds' is the icing on the cake when it comes to developing inner peace within our peaceful school. I remember driving back from a conference where a professor had expressed his concerns about the number of children who suffer from mental health issues not getting the appropriate intervention and support they need. During my journey, I was actually developing a vision for what we wanted to create as a school. In my view, mental health was clearly equal in weighting to addressing the physical health of our children. I remember thinking about how many of our children lacked skills of resilience and real life skills.

As a leadership team, we researched and developed a range of therapies, which we could deliver in-house without the waiting for referral processes of outside agencies. We created a space that is now called the 'Wellbeing Hub'. Children are selected across the school to take part in therapies depending on their individual needs. Staff are trained to deliver the therapies. These include Sand Tray Therapy, Music Therapy, Lego Therapy, Water Play, Sensory Circuits, Draw and Talk Therapy, Sensory Play and Cognitive Behavioural Therapy. Assessments are completed on entry and exit so we can measure their SEMH progress and identify whether some children need further intervention. Initially, when we implemented the therapies to enhance our 'Nurture Group', we had a significantly high number of safeguarding referrals as children were disclosing information that had previously been unknown to us. Twelve months later, we have now seen a reduction in referrals and a huge impact on the children who have accessed therapies. The Wellbeing Hub is open at lunchtimes and breaktimes for children to come and reflect on their behaviour before they find themselves in a situation they would not want to be in. We also run a lunchtime club for children to access Minecraft, where they can develop their own worlds, including a safe, happy and caring world.

Success and impact

For us at BPS, the impact of developing inner peace has resulted in a truly successful peaceful school. By prioritising the children's social, emotional and mental health and wellbeing, we have been able to develop confident and resilient learners. This has impacted on our whole school attainment and progress. During our Ofsted inspection, we were recognised for our work: 'The school's work to promote pupils' personal development and welfare is outstanding.'[2]

Concluding thoughts

Our journey for developing inner peace has been one of constant review, reflection and improvement and as a result we are now part of a proud, peaceful school community!

---

2   https://reports.ofsted.gov.uk/inspection-reports/find-inspection-report/provider/ ELS/103981. Accessed 15 January 2018.

CHAPTER 3

PEACEFUL PSHCE

David Holmes

Introduction

As a primary school teacher, headteacher and schools advisor for 30 years, I have had the privilege of working with a wide range of pupils, parents, governors, teachers and other professionals. I have seen numerous initiatives introduced and a whole raft of curriculum changes. Through all of this, I have held in my heart these wise words of advice from someone who mentored me at the start of my teaching career: 'David, remember this – you do not teach subjects, you teach children!' Subsequent experiences have made me realise how true that is and have fuelled my passionate belief in the importance of respecting the child, recognising all that children are capable of and my commitment to seeing children as my partners in education – we do it together! It is often said that we should 'give' children a voice in schools but as one young child said to me in response to that, 'What is given can be taken away!' Every child already has a voice, we just need to nurture and help develop it rather than squash it as schools did in the past.

Education, as the dictionary says, is 'an enlightening experience'. Experiences must be at the heart of what we do. They are what the children remember. At the heart of those experiences must be the ways in which we help them on their journey of living life to its fullest – life filled with the one thing we should all want everyone to know – PEACE! I have been part of the Peaceful Schools Movement since its inception in 2012 and a member of the Peaceful Schools Strategy Group.

So, what is this chapter all about? It takes a look at what schools are required to deliver in terms of the national curriculum for primary schools and sets that in the context of what it can mean to be a peaceful school. In order to do that, we will have a quick look at what is meant by 'peace' before going on to look in more detail about how we can approach Personal, Social, Health and Citizenship Education (PSHCE) from a peaceful perspective.

Personal, Social, Health and Citizenship Education

PSHCE is at the heart of the national curriculum for all primary school children and one of the key vehicles by which schools can meet their aims of:

- meeting National Curriculum requirements in relation to Social, Moral, Spiritual and Cultural Education (SMSC) and British values

- putting into practice their ethos and values

- implementing the United Nations Convention on the Rights of the Child (UNCRC)

- being judged favourably against Ofsted's Common Inspection Framework.

I say that PSHCE is only 'one of the vehicles' because PSHCE should not stand alone in helping schools meet these aims. To be successful, PSHCE needs to form part of a wider, holistic approach that:

- has complementary and reinforcing expectations and practices across all aspects of school life, teaching and learning

- is part of an integrated network of teaching and learning across different areas of the curriculum

- sees education as an ongoing journey of life and learning experiences

- seeks to equip children to meet life and learning to their fullest.

My concept of 'Peaceful PSHCE'

The National Curriculum requires all schools to use their PSHCE programme of education to equip pupils with a sound understanding of risk and with the knowledge and skills necessary to make safe and informed decisions. Peaceful PSHCE is about doing just that by promoting children's understanding of peace. It provides them with ongoing opportunities to experience peace in their lives both in and outside school through the ways in which we approach PSHCE teaching and learning, as well as many other aspects of school life.

This is not just about 'doing peace education'. Of course, peace education may well be part of the school's Peaceful PSHCE framework. My belief is that peaceful schools will have peace at the heart of all aspects of teaching, learning and school life because their senior leadership teams will believe in the importance of peace and will be committed to developing and sustaining a peaceful learning community. In peaceful schools, we should be able to observe that young people share that commitment to peace because of the peace they have experienced in the school.

What is peace?

In order to take a fresh look at PSHCE and make it into Peaceful PSHCE, there needs to be a shared understanding of what we mean by peace within the school. Children and adults all have different thoughts and ideas about what peace means and it is important to respect that. Members of the school community need to go through a process of consultation and discussion to arrive at a shared understanding of peace. Then they need to agree to commit to working for peace, as fully as they are able to do so in their different ways. This may take time, but it will be time well spent. I once did an activity with a group of teachers around the meaning of peace and we managed to fill six sides of flipchart paper with different ideas! We then somehow managed to pull these ideas into a definition that everyone felt they could own.

It is not my intention to present a definitive meaning of peace, just to suggest that peace has four interconnected strands:

- the state and nature of ourselves as individuals

- the nature of our relationships with others

- the state and nature of our community

- the nature of relationships between communities.

In my view, peace is not an all-or-nothing concept and it is both simple and complex! It has fluidity of strength, duration and impact. Peace is something that can 'just be there' in ways that we cannot articulate and yet, at the same time, peace can be nurtured, worked on, developed but also challenged, undermined and broken. Peace is a value, an experience and a belief. It can be momentary or lasting experiences that come in a whole range of ways, both individually and collectively.

Four levels of peace

My four strands are very much the same as the Peaceful Schools Movement's four-level approach to looking at peace in schools:

- personal or inner peace

- peaceful relationships

- peaceful communities

- global peace.

It is worth noting at this point that these are not stand-alone features of peace but are interconnected and interdependent areas throughout our lives, and that global peace is not an add-on but an integral offshoot of understanding what the other three are about.

A peaceful perspective

So, how do we approach PSHCE from a peaceful perspective? We need to think about how we can fill the PSHCE curriculum with peace. There are already so many excellent schemes of PSHCE work and approaches that are being used to great effect. To have Peaceful PSHCE, you do not need to replace them, instead hold fast to all that is good and all that meets the needs of your children, but look at what you do differently. Look through 'peaceful' eyes so that you can mould, modify and come to them in ways that enable to you to draw out the four levels or strands of peace so that the children's understanding and experiencing of peace can grow through them. Fill them with peace!

Start with an audit

As with many things, an audit is a good place to start looking at how peaceful the school is. What value does the school put on peace in all its aspects? School leaders need to take a holistic look at everything that happens in their school to make sure that children can experience peace in all aspects of school life, not just during Peaceful PSHCE.

The children in our care will only have successful Peaceful PSHCE if there is consistency across the curriculum, teaching and school life. How well is the PSHCE curriculum supported by the school's ethos, practices and expectations? Does peace permeate everything about the school – the policies, relationships, teaching approaches, expectations and the ways in which they are implemented and reinforced.

The following questions are offered as a possible starting point for that:

- Why do we want peaceful PSHCE?

- What are we doing now in PSHCE?

- How well does it link to, and develop, the four different aspects of peace?

- Do children and adults understand the links between different aspects of PSHCE and peace?

- Does school life promote Peaceful PSHCE?

From such an audit can come a picture of where the school is at – usually much stronger and closer to Peaceful PSHCE than we might at first think, and from there comes a way forward.

One of the things we did as a school was to turn our school rules into positively worded peace promises. For example, 'I promise to do all I can to make our school a peaceful place.' Staff, pupils and governors worked on this together because we wanted everyone to share responsibility for the creation of a peaceful school.

Making links

The key to the development of a successful peaceful approach to PSHCE is understanding the link between different topics or areas of PSHCE study and peace. For example, work done on anti-bullying is about peace. Anti-bullying work will help to make children peaceful and will create a peaceful school community. Part of the Derbyshire Healthy Schools work that I was involved in was to support anti-bullying projects in schools. After one such session with a group of Key Stage 1 children, a boy said to me: 'It's good this is, because if we can help bullies be peaceful inside, then they won't bully again.' He saw the connection! Developing an understanding of bullying, and the ways in which we respond to it, can reduce risks by helping the children to make informed decisions. It also helps to promote inner peace and peaceful relationships.

The work that children do learning about their bodies is another example of where there are natural links with peace. If children have an understanding of things like how their body works and the process of growing up, then they have a chance to be more at peace within themselves because this reduces the worries that children can have from not knowing and not understanding their bodies and what is happening.

Another example is drug education. Giving pupils the opportunity to develop their knowledge of substance misuse and helping them to acquire the attitudes, values and skills needed to understand the risks involved and make informed, safe decisions can help to promote both inner peace and peaceful relationships.

These are just three examples, but hopefully they give an indication of the ways in which we can fill what we are already doing with peace! The links are countless, so look for them and then explore how you can help the children make those links for themselves, remembering that they need to have an awareness of what they are being invited to understand, experience and take forward in and for themselves.

Values-based Education

Approaching PSHCE and Spiritual, Moral, Social and Cultural Education (SMSC) from a Values-based Education perspective is now being adopted very successfully by many schools. Such an approach offers a bold way of approaching Peaceful PSHCE as it starts by looking at those things that drive, motivate and fuel what we do – something that we perhaps shied away from for many years.

Peace will be an obvious value that would be incorporated into the list of values that we want our children to explore, experience and hopefully adopt for themselves. As a peaceful school, we might want to place a greater focus on the value of peace and think about how it underpins, and is a part of, other positive values. A quick look at the values being focused on by primary schools reveals such things as: care, tolerance, empathy, hope, optimism, friendship, unity – all of which have peace at the heart of them. Peaceful PSHCE and Values-based Education work well together.

The United Nations Convention on the Rights of the Child

The United Nations Convention on the Rights of the Child (UNCRC) is another important element in the promotion of Peaceful PSHCE. I strongly believe that the UNCRC is of vital importance to the lives of our children and young people. The Convention's articles, ethos, values and requirements impact directly on children's lives not only at a strategic planning or over-arching level but also in a real day-to-day sense.

The Convention underpins many aspects of government policy for children and plays a key role in determining good practice at all levels of working. It is the driving force for most young people-focused agencies, nationally and locally, both statutory agencies and those in the voluntary sector. Within the context of education, it is also firmly embedded in the National Curriculum through PSHCE.

Given its importance to all children, we must give our children and young people opportunities to explore and reflect on the Convention and its meaning for themselves and their peers around the world. As with other aspects of PSHCE, it is directly linked to the promotion of peace for the individual, for relationships, communities and by extension the world. Whilst no PSHCE programme can teach about all the articles in the UNCRC (there are over 50) their essence and purpose can be adopted and incorporated into what we are doing. That essence and purpose can be identified as follows.

All children having the right to:

- be treated in the same fair way

- go to school

- be the special person that they are

- have a say in things that affect them

- keep some things private

- food and clean water

- live in a clean and safe place

- be part of a caring family

- be kept safe and well

- be a child.

It is through these rights and responsibilities that peace can be promoted. For example, knowing that I have the right to keep some things private, should make me feel it is my responsibility to respect other people's privacy, and this can help to make me feel safe and secure, and through that, to be at greater peace. Understanding how and why other children might not benefit from the same rights as children have in this country can be a powerful force in developing a child's empathy with others around the world and motivating them to become peacebuilders.

On its own, the UNCRC does not form a comprehensive PSHCE scheme of work that will meet requirements and it cannot be the sole generator of peace in our young people. It does, however, offer another strand to both of them and is something that we should not let our young people miss out on.

British values

The teaching of so-called 'British Values' now forms another key element of all PSHCE. There is now a statutory requirement that these must be covered within the curriculum. Looking at them closely, it will be seen that many of these support the concept of peace for both the individual and communities. For example, one of the values that we have to teach is an appreciation that living under the rule of law protects individual citizens and is essential for well-being and safety. Protection, well-being and safety are words connected with peace for ourselves and others – to know that a vital prerequisite for experiencing peace is feeling safe and protected. The values of mutual respect and tolerance of those with different faiths and beliefs are also vital to the development of peaceful communities.

In exploring how we might develop Peaceful PSHCE and British Values, it is worth thinking of those values, not as a single group but as several groups, each with a different focus. For example:

- respect for other people – *example: empathy, positive global interdependence and self-understanding through positive diversity*

- the law – *example: the rule of law*

- society – *example: understanding how they can contribute positively to the lives of others locally and in a wider context*

- relationships – *example: respect for other people*

- the self – *example: self-knowledge, esteem and confidence.*

British values can be integrated into different areas of the PSHCE curriculum and explored as part of an existing framework. They can also be approached as a stand-alone teaching unit with a scheme of work or framework. But, however they are approached, it is important that we do not force links as can so easily happen in our striving to provide our young people with an integrated curriculum. PSHCE and the way in which we deliver it should reflect the way in which life, values and experiences interweave, but it should not do so at the expense of learning about and understanding individual parts of that weaving. It can be right and appropriate to keep parts separate.

For example, there is a requirement that our children have an understanding of how citizens can influence decision-making through democratic processes. Whilst there is a link with being peaceful, peaceful relationships and peaceful communities in this value, I believe that what is important here is their understanding of decision-making and democratic processes. We must not lose sight of that in our planning and the interconnecting of ideas for the convenience of an integrated curriculum or a peaceful focus. A few years ago, one of the Derbyshire primary schools opted to move from having a school council to having elected school ministers with different areas of responsibility, and on visiting them I was met by the Minister for Peace, who explained how she had been elected to promote peace in the school and that their latest project was a pupil audit of 'un-peaceful' places around the school and why they were like that. When I returned a few months later, that same minister took me round the school, explaining what they had changed and why, because, as she said, 'We all need a bit of peace in school, don't we Mr!'

Sex and Relationships Education

Sex and Relationships Education (SRE) very often forms another part of successful PSHCE teaching in primary schools. Unfortunately, our perceptions of what this area of learning can be is coloured by the strong views that some people have on the sex education element within it. This is unfortunate because we then miss appreciating the wonderful work being done on self-understanding, relationships, personal growth and emotional development through it. SRE also has many natural links with the promotion of inner peace and peaceful relationships and offers many opportunities to develop them.

Religious Education

How well do we make the connections between Religious Education (RE) and the four elements of peace? I suspect that the answer is: 'Quite well.' As with PSHCE, RE is approached in different ways by schools through the locally agreed syllabus or through the materials devised by different faiths. Most of them have strong links with PSHCE and of course peace. We need to ask ourselves about the way in which we look at what we do. Is there simply an emphasis on learning about each faith's beliefs, practices, symbols and stories or do we look at them from a peaceful perspective? Both approaches are perfectly compatible, and the balance of our approach should reflect what those faiths are about and how they impact on us as peace-seeking people. We could ask ourselves whether RE in our school develops children who know about faith and faiths, or whether it also helps our children to grow as peaceful people.

As with the reflection on how we might or might not integrate all aspects of British Values into a thematic curriculum, RE teaching and learning must hold true to the essence of what its aims are and not lose sight of them by bringing things together into a tenuous 'whole' for the sake of promoting a peaceful approach to all that we do.

So, we can make the journey to Peaceful PSHCE. Peace is everywhere in the curriculum and can be found in all sorts of places if we want to make the links. As I have already explained in this chapter, filling the curriculum and school with peace does not mean starting from scratch! It is about looking at what we do through peace-focused eyes so that we can find and draw out the peaceful aspects within and between topics in order for children to see them, and therefore understand and experience peace more fully through the curriculum.

An alternative, more radical, approach!

You may be interested to know that I have also developed an alternative and more radical approach to creating Peaceful PSHCE. This might appeal to some people. Instead of 'filling' PSHCE with peace, we can start with the four areas of peace as foundation or core and then exploring how PSHCE can be a part of them. It is my 4P approach – Peaceful People, Places and Participation.

'Peaceful People' focuses on how we can develop children's inner peace and peaceful relationships. 'Places' focuses on a peaceful community and global peace, although there is, of course, a crossover between them all. 'Participation' runs across all of them as it looks more at the how and why we do things. That is not to say that it is not about inner or personal peace because hopefully peaceful participation becomes internalised and part of their personal values.

The 4P approach stresses the positive by its focus on understanding, experiencing and valuing peace but also uses 'non-peace' as a part of that process. I believe that by recognising how, why and when we are not at peace, we can better develop our understanding of how and when we are at peace. I believe that it is important that both strands are followed as the real world and life are full of non-peaceful times and experiences, and our children need to be able to recognise these to keep themselves safe and to develop skills to bring peace to situations.

How, then, do we make the 4P journey of PSHCE?

Start from the four different aspects of peace: personal peace, peaceful relationships, peaceful communities and global peace. Think about what is meant by them and then identify the knowledge, skills, values, experiences and understanding needed to help the children grow in them. What, for example, do we believe the children need to have in terms of those things in order to take their inner peace forward? Self-understanding is, of course, a key player in relation to this so what do we do to help the children with that? Understanding themselves physically is there too, so how can we use an understanding of their bodies to help them feel good and positive and so generate opportunities to experience personal peace? Two examples of the ways in which PSHCE can promote peace – the curriculum expectations are full of them!

Peaceful relations and communities can be developed by showing and enabling the children to be with each other and to work together in different situations that allow for peaceful disagreement. Values like respect and empathy are needed in such situations. Giving the children access to learning about what is needed to create and sustain a wide variety of real and practical peaceful relationships and communities will inevitably lead to different forms of peaceful participation as well. Each Friday, I would do 'In the News' with my Year 5/6 class. Pupils took turns to lead a discussion about something that they had seen or heard in the news that week. We had some heated debates, but as one pupil told the Ofsted Inspector when being questioned about people falling out: 'You can disagree without falling out, you know.'

Hopefully, from these examples, it is becoming clear that this alternative approach is not about reinventing the wheel. It is about where we are coming from and why. It is about restructuring what we do because we want peace, and not PSHCE, to be at the heart of the curriculum.

Instead of looking at how British Values reflect peace, we ask how peace is promoted by our common values. Why and how, for example, do respect and the rule of law help me to experience inner peace and life in and as part of a peaceful community? How does democracy link to the valuing of peaceful decision-making and where do we find peace in and through the valuing of diversity?

Instead of structuring the curriculum year around different values, structure it around the different aspects of peace and then focus on how different ones can support and promote them, for example, peace through our rights, respect and responsibility.

The exploration of 4P could be used to develop understanding of the local community as the area of study, but explore it in terms of peace through questions such as:

- What makes it a peaceful place?

- Where are the non-peaceful spots?

- What values are needed for a peaceful community?

- How do people support each other and why?

- How can a common bond be found within it through the positivity of difference and diversity?

- How are decisions made and is that a peaceful process?

In order to begin answering any of those questions, the children will need to find out all about their community. They will need to understand that any community is a living, growing entity that has a history, a present and a future.

Again, it will be neither possible nor appropriate to tie all aspects of the curriculum into an integrated peaceful whole. Some things will need to maintain a level of learning independence in order to retain their integrity such as aspects of RE and elements of SRE. The 4P approach simply offers another way of creating an appropriately integrated curriculum. It is the reasoning underpinning our approach to the curriculum that is different.

The 4P SMSC education is a new way of organising and seeing the curriculum. It is an exciting and challenging approach that can, and perhaps should, be at the heart of a school being a peaceful school. As with all ways of meeting the National Curriculum requirements around SMSC, the 4P approach needs to go beyond lesson time and into the whole of school life. How well do those structures and processes support them? Is there a partnership between adults and children? Do you have a School Council or a Peaceful School Council with, perhaps, Ministers for Peace on it? How well does the school environment – physically, emotionally and spiritually – reflect and enable the children to experience the different aspects of peace that we are trying to help them grow in?

Assessment

Assessing pupils' progress in PSHCE has always been a challenge, given its involvement with values, skills and ways of living that are personal and that can be displayed to varying degrees, depending on circumstances, group dynamics and time. This does not mean that we cannot assess PSHCE, we can endeavour to do so with rigour and clarity. We can aim to evaluate the quality and impact of what we have been doing with the children, the time spent on it, and the energy and resources given over to it.

Peaceful approaches to PSHCE and the ways in which we develop the children's SMSC education give us an opportunity to take a new perspective on the assessment process. At a whole school level, there needs to be regular and objective assessment of how well the curriculum framework and teaching and learning reflect, enhance and support the school's peaceful values, ethos and culture. We then need to assess the experiences and opportunities that we have given our children during and through PSHCE/SMSC education. How well have we:

- given the children appropriate opportunities to learn, develop skills, experience, understand, grow and develop in relation to the four different aspects of peace

- used appropriate and relevant resources

- given them time and the skills needed for self-reflection and understanding

- recognised and reinforced their developing social, moral, spiritual and cultural maturity

- integrated PSHCE/SMSC with school and out-of-school life?

All of which can be done using a whole range of techniques, including self-evaluation and reflection combined with ongoing observation and the noting of when children display or share peaceful values, behaviours, skills and understanding in the context of inner peace, peaceful relationships, being part of a peaceful community and global peace, along with some of the more specific things that schools are required to evidence.

Ofsted

The school inspection process has, and will continue to establish, the framework and criteria by which PSHCE is judged. A peaceful approach to PSHCE can go a long way towards evidencing those judgements and justifying what is being done towards personal development and the school culture. Much of the evidence base required by Ofsted falls within the remit of a peaceful approach. Schools need to ensure that what they are doing peacefully has clearly identifiable aims and structure with a teaching and learning framework that ensures rigour of approach, continuity and progression.

Outcomes and challenges

Being a peaceful school, and introducing a peace-focused approach to the development of PSHCE has the potential to present a number of challenges. It can require a culture change and this takes time. Some staff, parents, governors and even children may initially feel uncertain or uncomfortable with some of the changes that are being made and may resist them. This is particularly pertinent when the reasons for doing so are not shared or owned. It all takes time, planning and reasoning – much of which needs to happen at senior management level so that everyone can be as ready as possible for the wonderful educational journey that it can take us on. It is a journey and change that we also have to be ready to justify to Ofsted. This can also be a challenge when the peace-versus-raised-attainment relationship is not easily observable or quantifiable. The link is that, if pupils are able to be at peace within themselves and able to learn in a safe and peaceful environment (physical, social, emotional and spiritual), then they are more likely to come to school positively and be in a better place within themselves to learn – we teach children not subjects!

Schools offer young people a unique environment that can provide the calm, the peace and the security that the rest of the world does not always offer. A boy I once taught found himself in a challenging personal situation when his parents separated. Mum and Dad came in to talk to me about moving him because it was becoming difficult to get him to school as they had both moved out of the area. His response to them was simple: 'You got us into this mess, not me – I am staying here, this is the one place where I know where I am – sort it!' That is why we need to rise to the challenge!

Conclusion

Peaceful PSHCE, either as peace-filled PSHCE or in the form of the 4Ps, needs to be at the heart of our schools if we are to successfully take the children and ourselves on the journey of being more and more peacefully participating people and places. It starts as a state of mind – the valuing of peace and the belief that it is the fundamental right of everyone to be able to experience peace. It is a right that brings us, as those in a position to influence and affect young people's lives through their education, the responsibility of being committed to exploring all the ways in which that right can happen in real and meaningful ways.

Peaceful PSHCE will not achieve that on its own, but it can be a major player in that process. So, let us fill what we already do with peace, or better still, let us turn the world around and explore how we can use what is there to be done to promote those four things that are at the heart of fulfilled, world-changing young people: inner peace, peaceful relationships, peaceful communities and their belief in, and determination to work for, global peace.

Further Reading

Department for Education (DfE) (2014) *The National Curriculum in England: Framework for Key Stages 1–4*. London: DfE.

Department for Education (2015) *The National Curriculum in England: Primary Curriculum*. London: DfE.

Department for Education (2015) *Promoting Fundamental British Values as Part of SMCS in Schools*. London: DfE.

Holmes, D. (2012) *Promoting the Spiritual Health and Well-being of Children in Primary Schools*. Hampshire: Spiritual England.

Holmes, D. (2013) *Pathways for Peaceful Schools*. Hampshire: Spiritual England.

Holmes, D. (2014) *Our Schools – Building a Culture of Partnership and Participation*. Hampshire: Spiritual England.

Holmes, D. (2014) *Peaceful PSHCE*. Hampshire: Spiritual England.

Ofsted (2014, updated 2016) *Ofsted Inspection of Maintained Schools*. London: Ofsted.

Ofsted (2015) *School Inspection Handbook*. London: Ofsted.

Ofsted (2015) *The Common Inspection Framework: Education, Skills and Early Years*. London: Ofsted.

Ofsted (2016) *How Ofsted Inspects Maintained Schools and Academies*. London: Ofsted.

PSHE Association (2017) *PSHE Programme of Study Key Stages 1–5*.

UN (1989) *The United Nations Convention on the Rights of the Child*.

CHAPTER 4

PEACEFUL RELATIONSHIPS IN PRIMARY SCHOOLS

Jackie Zammit

Introduction

The West Midlands Quaker Peace Education Project, known as 'Peacemakers', is an educational charity that has been working with schools for 30 years. I have been a peace education trainer with Peacemakers since 2011, starting on a freelance basis and now part of the staff team. I came to peace education through my experience within the development education sector.

My passion and belief in the role that education can play in building a more peaceful and resilient society has evolved from my personal experiences at home and school. When I was growing up, inner peace was elusive and feelings of fear, anxiety, distrust, loneliness and sadness were 'normal' to me. Opportunities to explore or counter these feelings were not readily available. Much later, I came to realise that those early experiences and feelings had affected my ability to learn and my ability to think creatively and decisively.

My daughter and son both experienced Peacemaker courses at primary school and were peer mediators. It was through them that I decided to find out more about the work. I learned that the organisation was supporting my children to become more emotionally literate, self-aware, empathic and confident within a school ethos that was allowing them to flourish as people, as well as to achieve academically. I believe that this positive experience of school and the relationships that my children built both with their friends and staff has helped, and continues to help, them to navigate life's challenges.

Being able to play a part in supporting other young people in this way, offering opportunities to experience alternative viewpoints and choices, is a real privilege.

Peacemakers offers courses and resources for schools. This chapter shares some of the foundations for peace on which our work is based and then considers the practical approaches that we use in school for whole class, child and adult learning.

Educating for peace

> *Ensure that children, from an early age, benefit from education on the values, attitudes, modes of behaviour and ways of life, to enable them to resolve any dispute peacefully and in a spirit of respect for human dignity and of tolerance and non-discrimination.*

> Declaration and Programme of Action
> on a Culture of Peace (1999)[1]

Education has a significant role to play in building a culture of peace in our communities and the wider world. Primary school children spend almost half a year in the company of children to whom they mainly have no familial connection. They share space and time with children older and younger than themselves, who may look different to themselves, from families with similar or different values and beliefs. They also share this space and their time with adults who bring their own experiences, values and attitudes into the school with them. It is not surprising that in these communities, whilst deep relationships may be formed that can last a lifetime, many relationships will be tested. Conflicts will always be an inevitable part of life, including school life, and yet they can still surprise us and catch us out.

The 'them and us' barrier to peace

One very significant barrier to developing peaceful relationships is through the use of the word 'they' to describe people in our schools, often attached to a blaming word, when things are not working.

---

1   UN General Assembly Resolution 54/243. Declaration and Programme of Action on a Culture of Peace (1999) B.9. *Actions to Foster a Culture of Peace through Education.*

'They (the parents) never want to get involved' or 'They (the lunchtime supervisors) always pass the problem back to us' or 'There's no point discussing it with them, they (the Senior Leadership Team) just don't listen' or 'They (the class) are so fussy.' Building peaceful relationships is about recognising the barriers between 'us' and 'them' and starting to break them down. It is not about eliminating conflict but about learning how to handle it well, so that when a 'them and us' situation arises we can ask what are 'we' going to do to put things right.

Educating for peace can equip children and adults with the skills they need to deal with conflict creatively. It is essential if we are to find alternative responses to violence and exerting power. We need to recognise that schools can be violent places in ways that are visible and invisible, which can be in the form of direct violence, cultural violence and structural violence (Galtung 1990).

Building positive peace

Building a school culture based on positive peace can help mitigate both visible and invisible violence. Positive peace has been described as 'creating the optimum environment for human potential to flourish' (Institute of Economics and Peace 2016). It is about working hard so as to ensure that attitudes and values such as justice, fairness, equality, equity, inclusion and a sense of belonging exist in every corner of our classrooms. It goes further than the notion of peace as the absence of violence. This notion of positive peace and human flourishing informs the work of Peacemakers. By supporting children and adults in schools to directly engage with the attitudes and values of positive peace, explore them and challenge thinking around them, a context is created by which the knowledge and skills to develop peaceful relationships can be created.

Examples of negative peace may be to separate two children who have fallen out and contain them in different parts of the playground, or to ban football because it is the cause of too many arguments. In a school that advocates positive peace, children would be encouraged to explore what is happening for them at these times, to discuss who is being affected and to work with each other and/or with staff to come up with a solution. When things are going well, they would learn the skills to resolve conflicts and develop social and emotional attributes that help them to weather challenging experiences, so that when things go wrong, they have a strong foundation on which to repair any harm. This approach can work! It can start with one class and, at its most successful, it becomes part of the fabric of the school.

Whole class learning

How can teachers deepen the relationships with and within their classroom so they are resilient enough to weather change, withstand disagreements and build a strong sense of belonging? Dedicating time to focus on relationships can help achieve this. Peacemakers' courses typically run over ten weeks. We spend an afternoon a week with a year group over this time, working with the class to deepen relationships, develop social and emotional skills, and learn about peace and conflict. Peacemakers has designed a curriculum (West Midlands Quaker Peace Education Project 2014) that results in a classroom with positive peace at its heart.

Regular time and space just to learn the skills to build, maintain and repair relationships can have a long-term impact on class behaviour, friendships and ultimately on academic learning. Our experience tells us, however, that if the learning and opportunity to practice is confined to just these ten weeks then the impact, perhaps obviously, will be minimal. So we try to work with staff during the Peacemakers course, recognising that they will be bringing with them their experience of the class and possibly previous knowledge of working in circles and of social and emotional learning. One measure of success for us is when teachers take the approaches and ideas and run with them, continuing the work long after we leave.

But what are we going to do?

This is a common question. We are passionate about working with the whole class in a circle and this can create some concerns for teachers. They may worry about running out of ideas with regular circle time; their own lack of experience of running circles with Key Stage 2; about how children with special needs will be involved; or about the assumption that we get together because there is a problem.

The circle, when constructed thoughtfully, beautifully reflects the values of positive peace. When the chairs are the same and everyone in the class – including all the adults and children – is in the circle, the space reflects the values of equity, fairness and inclusion. The space can be used in different ways and for different purposes. Traditionally, circle time has been used for dialogue and discussion, hence the popular notion of circle time as being only about 'talking about our problems'. However, circle time can also be used for games, drama, pair work and group work. Chairs can easily be rearranged to create different spaces and then brought back together into a circle.

Sessions are planned with a focus on skills practice. Here are the kinds of skills needed to form resilient relationships in the classroom:

Participation	Reflection	Empathy
Creative Thinking	Listening	Cooperation
Taking responsibility	Collaboration	Communication
Managing feelings and emotions	Conflict resolution	Critical Thinking
Concentration	Affirmation	

Children will be practicing these skills through different parts of their everyday curriculum, but often these are secondary to the subject being taught. For example, if we ask children to work in a small group on a science task, such as building a simple circuit with a light bulb, battery and electrical wire, we are expecting them to collaborate as well as developing their science knowledge. The children need to work together to solve a problem. But what happens if they are unable to collaborate? What happens if children refuse to share or can't agree on how to solve the problem? Do we impose sanctions for poor behaviour? Do we work around the issue by only allowing children to work with the people we know they can work with? There is evidence to suggest that learning the skills to cooperate and collaborate with anyone in the class can help lead to better learning outcomes (Kutnick and Kington 2006). A session to practice collaboration skills might look like this example in the box below.

Check-in: Use this time to settle the class into the circle and get to know each other better. A talking piece (this can be any object) is passed around and everyone gets the chance to respond to a question such as: 'Please tell us one way in which you have helped someone this week.'

Game: Use games to mix up the group and work together, for example 'Birthday Round'. The class sit themselves in the circle in the order of their birthdays. Adults cannot help, but they must be included. Children invite them to sit in the correct place in the circle.

Activity: Any problem-solving activity that involves working in small groups. You could arrange strips of card with pictures in the correct order to tell a story and then use role play to act it out.

Reflect and review (all together): Here are examples of questions that could be discussed in the circle: On a scale of 1–5, how would you rate your group's ability to work together to complete the task? What skills did we use? What was easy/difficult about these tasks? What is collaboration and cooperation? At what other times do we need to collaborate or cooperate?

Affirmation: End the session with an affirmation activity. You could randomly choose one person in the class and invite others to say why they appreciate that person.

Check-out: Every person can respond to a question like, 'What would help you to be able to collaborate with someone in the class who you don't normally work with?'

Regular sessions like these help children to feel comfortable with one another. For some classes, it may take several sessions before changes are noticed.

Learning agreements

A learning agreement at the start of a series of circle sessions can be useful. Putting this agreement in place with children after two or three sessions leads to a more meaningful discussion of what we can expect from one another. This is because, after two or three sessions, the children will know what to expect during this time, and they will have more information on which to base their suggestions for the learning agreement.

Forming an agreement based on the needs of the group works particularly well. We try to understand the children's hidden/unseen needs that might be causing certain emotions and feelings which may be affecting the behaviour that we see. The child's unmet need may be a sense of belonging, to be included or to be listened to (Hopkins 2003).

To form an agreement based on needs, a set of cards can be used. Cards with emotional needs, such as safety, friendship, support, respect and reassurance, are placed in the centre of the circle and each need is explained to the class where appropriate. We ask the class, 'What do you need from each other to be successful in Peacemakers?' Pupils and adults place counters on one or more needs that are most important to them. From this, an agreement can be discussed that takes into account the needs of the group. For example, a group of Year 5 pupils devised the following agreement shown in the box below.

In our Peacemakers sessions we agree to:

Reassure each other if things go wrong.

Encourage one another.

Include people if they are left out.

Try to build **trust** with one another.

Try to be **patient**.

Try to make new **friends**.

Support each other.

Be **kind** and make sure that no one gets emotionally hurt.

Listen to everyone.

The learning agreement is then referred to when things go wrong and when things go right. If a pupil is calling out rather than listening, we can go back to the agreement and ask, 'What's missing now from our circle?' or 'How do we feel about that?' or 'What can we do to help make things better?'

Sometimes, whole class dynamics can make us nervous to try something new. Developing a classroom ethos where we are working with children to find out what is happening with them takes courage on the part of the adults involved. The two scenarios below are based on the experience of our Peacemakers' trainers.

Scenario 1

Sometimes, we can be lulled into a false sense of security. The class will do everything you ask of them and more. The children participate, they discuss with each other, they have great ideas. And then, their class teacher is absent. The atmosphere changes. The children can completely flounder. They struggle to listen and be respectful to one another and they test the boundaries. That's when I realise that the 'good' behaviour for my benefit is not innate. The lid is taken off and real individuals emerge. When asked what is happening, children will say, 'We know we aren't going to get into trouble with you' or 'We know you aren't going to shout at us.' It's great when that happens, because then the deeper conversations can start!

Scenario 2

I remember working with a Year 4 class and it was early on in a ten-week course. We were seated in a circle. The session started calmly. We checked in, played a game and I explained what was going to happen. We then did group work and three children decided to go and sit under the tables. One of them, Jason, was banging the underside of the table, attracting a lot of attention from other children. I could see that the teacher was getting anxious. She was watching the door, hoping, she said later, that other adults weren't going to come into the room. I was getting anxious, too. I decided to play a game to bring us all back together. The first version of the game was competitive and the children really enjoyed it. The children from under the tables voluntarily came and joined in. Buoyed with renewed confidence, I decided to play the cooperative version of the game. I saw the smile slowly fall from Jason's face when he realised that there was to be no winner in this game. He was outraged at what he understood to be complete injustice. 'Why do we have to play this? It's not fair! What's the point? It's just stupid,' and with that he walked out of the classroom.

In both scenarios, the trainers involved put their trust in the process, helped by supportive school staff. The teacher in the second scenario was sceptical at first but came to trust the process, too. The children did stop going under the tables after a few sessions, and Jason successfully completed a cooperative game and got a round of applause! Most importantly, the ethos of the classroom started to change. Children slowly began to develop their social skills and became more confident that members of staff were genuine when trying to find out what was happening to them.

Child learning

> Abdul came to me one day and said, 'Sonya just took the hoop off me without asking!' He was upset, so I reminded him about our work in the Peacemakers sessions and asked him if there was anything he could try. He nodded, and confidently went over to Sonya while I observed from a slight distance and they resolved the argument. Abdul said, 'I didn't like it when you took the hoop off me.' Sonya replied, 'Sorry, I was just trying to tidy up because the bell had gone, I wasn't being mean.' I heard Abdul say, 'That's OK, I know why you did it now. Sorry for shouting at you when you did it.' They were sat at the same table that afternoon and went on to work peacefully together. (Year 3 teacher, Birmingham)

Young children benefit from having tools at their disposal to help build, maintain and repair their relationships. If we invest heavily in building and maintaining relationships then these can act as foundations on which relationships can more easily be repaired. This means equipping children with the vocabulary and the language they need along with the opportunity to put the skills they are learning into practice.

Building relationships

Building relationships means taking every opportunity for children to learn about each other, to make connections between one another, and to develop a natural curiosity and respect for the lives of others. When people are in a circle, their relationships are on show. Everyone can see each other. This is a different environment from learning at other times. Vulnerable relationships are more visible, as are those that are already strong. The circle provides a space for building confidence and self-esteem, getting to know each other and working outside of friendship groups. Encouraging respectful conversation is of paramount importance. This means taking turns and using each other's names as much as possible. In the following box are some examples of the types of skills that can be taught and practiced and also some of the kinds of conversations that we might hear.

The skill of getting to know each other in circle time
Examples of language from pupils:

'Ruby, have you ever been to...?'

'This is Thomas. He would like to be a cameraman one day.'

The skill of communication, especially active listening and speaking
Examples of language from pupils:

'I like your idea, Abdie, but I think...'

'I agree with Tom because...and I disagree with Aisha because...'

'Toby, have you thought about...?'

The skill of participation
Examples of language from pupils:

'I liked being in your group Reuben.'

The skill of affirmation
Examples of language from pupils:

'Sophie, we appreciate you in this class because you are...'

'It's good to be me because I am...'

The skill of reflection
Examples of language from pupils:

'I would give our group a 3 out of 5. We did well but we could do better next time by...'

It is not unusual for children to tell us that there are people in their class to whom they rarely, if ever, speak. Honesty is important when working in this way. We explain that we are not trying to make everyone become best friends but that our aim at this stage is for us to be able to get along with anyone in the class well enough to be able to complete a task together. Children enjoy the opportunity to 'check in' to the space. One pupil said, 'I like Peacemakers because it makes me feel calm and safe when we have the check-in.' Affirmation enables us to regularly celebrate the positive attributes of one another. Making this an experience where children are chosen at random helps to focus on everyone's good qualities, whatever has happened during the day.

Maintaining relationships

Maintaining relationships means keeping relationships healthy and mutually respectful. Developing a 'feelings vocabulary' can help pupils articulate what is happening for them at any particular time. Often, during a check-in, children will say that they feel 'normal' or 'OK' or they will pass the ball because they don't know what they are feeling. A brainstorm of all the words, colours and images that children can think of for different feeling words, usually generates a rich bank of words and pictures that children can draw on.

Here are some other words for 'nervous' from children in Year 4 and Year 5 classes: agitated, anxious, apprehension, blank, butterflies in my tummy, 'I can't do it,' confused, excited, fearful, 'feeling for…', frightened, frustrated, hesitating, nerve-wracking, not knowing what to say, petrified, puzzled, scared, shivering, shy, stage fright, suspicious, terrified, uncomfortable, unconfident, worried.

By encouraging self-reflection, children also develop empathy and understanding for how other people are feeling and can put the vocabulary into context. Teachers have told us that an in-depth exploration of feelings, looking at images of people showing a variety of emotions and using drama – to show those feelings – has the added benefit of improving children's achievements in literacy.

Drama can help children to role play different scenarios and practice different outcomes when the stakes are low. Drama techniques such as 'hot-seating' give an opportunity to practice different responses and see what happens.

Here are some examples of the kind of language we might hear when practicing the skills needed to maintain relationships.

The skill of being able to express and explain our own feelings, being empathic, developing confidence and self-esteem
Pupils have said:

'When my teacher tells me I have done well, I feel proud.'

'When my best friend is not at school, I feel anxious. I don't know who I am going to play with.'

'When I took the pencil from Ella, I think she felt annoyed.'

'I know we don't usually play with Layla, but I think we should ask her to play with us today.'

The skill of self-reflection and review
Pupils have said:

'I need to practice listening when other people are speaking.'

'I think the game wasn't very successful because some people were not following the rules.'

The skill of collaboration
Pupils have said:

'It was fun working with people I don't know very well.'

'I found it hard because some people in my group were not taking it seriously.'

The skill of creativity and using drama, games and play to take risks and try out new ideas
Pupils have said:

'When we acted out the argument, we tried to compromise to solve the problem.'

'We found three ways of solving the problem in our group!'

Repairing relationships

Repairing relationships means supporting each other to put things right when they go wrong. It is also about finding ways to make the relationship stronger and healthier. Children respond well to the idea of conflict being like an escalator – once you get on, it can be hard to get off. Escalators also come down as well as go up, so we can talk about de-escalation as well as escalation. Blame is one of the main contributing factors in conflict escalation. Once children learn what blame sounds like: 'She did it on purpose' or 'He's always taking my things' or 'It's all her fault,' they quickly learn to recognise it and verbalise what has happened in an argument. They start to have conversations that include the language below.

The skill of responding to conflict positively
Pupils have said:

'Miss, we went too far up the conflict escalator!'

'I used blaming language, but I didn't mean to.'

'I was angry, so I walked away.'

The skill of conflict resolution
Pupils have said:

'When I hear unkind words, I think to myself, "What did I do?" I feel confused.'

Sonya said, 'Sorry, I was just trying to tidy up because the bell had gone, I wasn't being mean.'

Abdul said, 'That's OK, I know why you did it now. Sorry for shouting at you when you did it.'

Another example: 'It was partly my fault.'

The skill of critical thinking
Pupils have asked and said:

'Tell me what happened?'

'What shall we do to put things right?'

'I've listened to you and now I've changed my mind.'

For relationships to be repaired, young people are supported to be able to actively listen, to empathise and to recognise the right time to work things out. De-escalation strategies like finding ways to compromise, take responsibility and manage complex emotions like anger are explicitly taught and practiced. Developing a greater sense of self-awareness helps young people to recognise what they need when things go wrong.

Adult learning

Adults who come into contact with children are acting as role models, all the time. The way in which we deal with situations when we are stressed, the tone of voice we use, the messages we convey through our body language, the words we use, the way in which we speak to lunchtime supervisors, parents, other children, are all teaching children how to behave in their relationships with adults and their peers:

Challenging behaviour is much less common where staff and learners enjoy positive relationships based on mutual respect and consideration. These strengths are supported and reinforced by a shared understanding and acceptance of the school's values. Staff get to know learners as individuals and respond to their differing personalities, circumstances and learning needs. This leads to a positive learning climate in individual classrooms and in the school in general. (HMIE 2010)

At Peacemakers, we believe that creating a positive classroom climate built on mutual respect takes concerted effort. It is about the teacher paying attention to the needs of everyone in the room and enabling an environment in which everyone takes care of one another. Like children, teachers can benefit from training to enable self-reflection and awareness, and to give them the tools and skills to be good communicators and to be able to facilitate and support positive relationships within their classrooms. The basic ingredients of a positive classroom climate as created by the adults in the room might be: attention to the physical space; modelling positive behaviour; developing conflict literacy; and working *with* children rather than doing *to* them.

Attention to physical space is arguably the easiest thing to get right! What does your classroom look like? Are there cups on the windowsill, books falling off the bookcase or a window blind that doesn't work? Research demonstrates that the learning environment affects the engagement, motivation, self-esteem, attendance, well-being and achievement of students. An attractive and well-looked-after classroom will help to support not only learning but also good relationships.

Modelling positive behaviour and developing conflict literacy are challenging for teachers, especially when they are stressed and class sizes are big. Through our staff training sessions, we at Peacemakers have seen that when teachers become more self-aware, they start to go through a process of transformation. Supporting colleagues through this process in a compassionate way can make the difference between this being a positive and a negative experience.

Circles for adults

We use the circle in staff training because it can act as a useful space for supporting this process of self-discovery and awareness. Approaches for dialogue and discussion used for children work just as well with adults. Some adults feel really comfortable working in this way, others need time to settle into the space. Once that has been achieved, we find that people participate and engage in ways they might not do had the session been structured in more traditional ways. Whether a staff meeting, team briefing, parent workshop or staff training, we are told time and again by adults that just being together in a positive environment is highly valued. Facilitating meeting spaces in this way is again modelling what we would like to happen in a classroom:

> As a new member of staff, this workshop has helped me build new relationships with other members of staff. I see people down this end of the school but not the other end, so the workshops and the games have been nice to get know people – it's been good. (Primary Teacher, Birmingham)

> The workshop was held in a warm and welcoming room, where you are not put under pressure to talk but soon find yourself interacting and relaxing. (Primary School Parent, Birmingham)

Transformation

I led some training many years ago on refugee issues. A deputy headteacher attended because a refugee had just enrolled in his school and he didn't know how to support her. We were in a room with teachers from schools where 40 or so different languages were being spoken in the playground and children were arriving and departing virtually every day. Part way through the day, the deputy headteacher became very quiet. I was concerned and so I sought him out over lunch. He explained that he had become overwhelmed. The children in his school, he felt, were not being exposed to other people's realities, and he felt that he had failed them. He could have left but he didn't. By the end of the day, he had re-engaged and explained to the group, 'I felt stuck. But it's only when you are in those stuck moments that you really begin to learn.' This phrase has stayed with me. It represents transformation. Whatever decisions he made following the training may be affected by that moment of transformation. Not only did he become self-aware, but he also stayed with that feeling, processed it in his own mind, shared it with colleagues and then made a decision about how he was going to act from then on.

Thinking about adults as role models encourages thinking about behaviour. Work developed within the restorative justice movement has identified that there are four types of responses to behaviour: punitive, neglectful, permissive and restorative (Wachtel 2012).

Working *with* children using a restorative approach

In terms of building and maintaining relationships, working *with* children and colleagues can reap the greatest benefits. Let's take a straightforward example and imagine that Kylie has not finished her Maths work. The bell is about to go and you have told the class that they must finish their work before break. A punitive response would be, 'You haven't finished your work Kylie. Now the whole class will have to wait until you are finished.' In terms of relationships, this could provoke a reaction from Kylie and escalate the situation; it also labels and shames Kylie in front of the class.

A neglectful response would be to ignore the fact that Kylie hasn't finished and not address it all. A permissive response would be, 'Kylie I can see that you haven't finished, you are really struggling aren't you, let me help you to…' This might get the work finished, but it is not addressing Kylie's underlying needs.

A restorative response might take place in the moment or could take place later. You might ask, 'Kylie, what was happening for you in Maths today? What was happening to you when I said the work needed to be done before break? What did you need? What shall we do about the work you haven't finished?' and so on. These kinds of questions can be modelled and practiced when working in a circle so that children become accustomed to hearing them. If a game goes wrong, then we can ask, 'What was happening for us during that game? What could we do to put it right?' By coming up with a solution to solve the problem together, you can find out what's happening for Kylie. The relationship can be maintained and a realistic solution can be found. When Kylie goes on to complete her work on time later in the week, a public show of support can raise her self-esteem:

> Teachers need to be aware of supportive or conflictive interactions that are visible and/or audible to the other students in the classroom. So, the combination of a private reprimand aimed at decreasing disruptive behaviour and a public expression of support another time might serve both classroom management and peer ecology, and thus individual students' development, best. (Hendrickx *et al.* 2016)

Finally, developing a shared language to talk about conflict and a space in which feelings can be conveyed can help relationships be repaired more quickly. When adults learn this language alongside children, understanding and assumptions can be explored. Sessions might include understanding conflict styles, exploring conflict escalation, understanding the role of blame, recognising the mixed emotions that people experience when in conflict, what to do to calm down when angry and so on.

Professionals working with teenagers and adults are often surprised at the depth of conversation that young children are able to engage in. There can be an assumption that primary children are too young to talk about these things. We have found that in Early Years and Foundation Stage there are lots of conversations about relationships. Children are encouraged to talk about themselves, their friends, their family and concepts like sharing. Less time seems to be given to this as children move up the school.

A peace education curriculum

We (Peacemakers) have published a resource called *Learning for Peace* (Zammit and Hagel 2016). It aims to support children's spiritual, moral, social and cultural development (SMSC) through educating for peace. The resource was published to enable any class teacher to regularly facilitate circles and we offer training that can run alongside it. It suggests a spiral curriculum from Reception to Year 6 and encourages the whole school to put time aside for it. Some schools are setting aside the same time every week for every class to focus on *Learning for Peace*. This is benefiting teachers' relationships with each other as well as with their pupils.

Sometimes, we find out from monitoring data that relationships between staff and children in school are stronger than relationships between staff. But should it always be 'just about the children'? Reflecting back to the beginning of this chapter, we are working within a system that can be structurally violent. There are systems and decisions being made beyond the school that affect staff but are made without them, and this can make schools stressful places to be in:

> The best thing for students is a happy, motivated staff. By putting the staff equal first with the students, you are doing the best you can do for the students. Any headteacher who claims she or he always puts students first probably hasn't thought through in detail exactly what that means. (Tomsett 2013)

A school that encourages all relationships to flourish is a school that cares deeply about the health and well-being of the whole school community.

Conclusion

Just as school buildings need maintaining in order to avoid costly repairs, so do relationships. The cost to morale, well-being and to school budgets of constantly needing to repair harm can be high. A school that enables all relationships to flourish, and is continually building and maintaining those relationships, is a school that cares deeply about the health and well-being of the whole school community.

And, finally, some encouraging feedback from a Year 4 teacher

Adam used to be very confrontational. He would run out of the classroom at various points in the day and he could go from 0 to 100 very quickly. When we started the Peacemaker course, he didn't want to participate. He left the circle, went under the table and made noises. I found it difficult to ignore him. But he joined in with the games and enjoyed them. As the weeks went on, I started noticing an improvement in class. He wasn't running out any more. He would still get stroppy sometimes, but I saw him start to participate. As time went on, I started to change my approach. I started to listen to him more and gave him more time. I became less concerned with having to fix things there and then. I had this written into his individual behaviour plan – that he needed space. When the course finished, I ran my own peace circle. His attitude had changed so much. He took responsibility for setting up the circle, he was ready and waiting to take part, and in the circle he reflected on how he was feeling, which was unusual for him. He really enjoyed it. Today, we have seen a breakthrough. He fell out with someone, but he didn't get cross. He didn't go from 0 to100 like he has done before. He didn't have a strop either, but he got on with his work. I told him how proud I am of him. I know he sometimes feels I'm getting at him. He craves attention. It feels good giving him this positive attention.

References

Galtung, J. (1990) 'Cultural violence.' *Journal of Peace Research 27*, 3, 291–305.

Hendrickx, M.M.H.G., Mainhard, M. T., Boor-Klip, H. J., Cillessen, A.H.M., Brekelmans, M. (2016) 'Social dynamics in the classroom: Teacher support and conflict and the peer ecology.' *Teaching and Teacher Education 53*, 30–40.

HM Inspectorate of Education (HMIE), Scotland (2010) 'Journey to excellence –learning together resource.' Accessed 27 November 2017 at www.shetland.gov.uk/education/documents/PromotPositiveRelationships.pdf.

Hopkins, B. (2003) *Just Schools: A Whole School Approach to Restorative Justice.* London: Jessica Kingsley Publishers.

Institute for Economics and Peace (2016) *Positive Peace Report: A Compilation of the Leading Research on Positive Peace and Resilience.*

Kutnick, P. and Kington, A. (2006) 'Children's friendships and learning in school: Cognitive enhancement through social interaction?' *ResearchGate, 75*, 4, 521–538.

Tomsett, J. (2013) 'How can headteachers and leaders promote staff well-being?' *The Guardian Leadership/Teacher's Blog.* Accessed 5 December 2017 at www.theguardian.com/teacher-network/teacher-blog/2013/jul/01/school-staff-wellbeing-headteacher-leaders.

Wachtel, T. (2012) 'Defining restorative.' International Institute for Restorative Practices. Accessed 27 November 2017 at www.iirp.edu/pdf/Defining-Restorative.pdf.

West Midlands Quaker Peace Education Project (2014) Peacemakers Curriculum. Accessed 5 December 2017 at www.peacemakers.org.uk/resources/learning-for-peace.

Zammit, J. and Hagel, S. (Eds) (2016) *Learning for Peace.* Leek: Lifeworlds Learning.

Further reading

Adams, L. 'Learning a new skill is easier said than done.' Gordon Training Institute. Accessed 27 November 2017 at http://www.gordontraining.com/free-workplace-articles/learning-a-new-skill-is-easier-said-than-done/#.

Morrison, B. (2007) *Restoring Safe School Communities.* Sydney: Federation Press.

Rutherford, G. 'What's wrong with pencils on the floor? Classroom environment and its impact on learning.' Accessed 27 November 2017 at http://www.wyche.worcs.sch.uk/Wyche%20Curriculum.htm.

United Nations (1999) 'Declaration and programme of action on a culture of peace.' Accessed 27 November 2017 at http://www.un-documents.net/a53r243.htm.

CHAPTER 5

PEACEFUL RELATIONSHIPS IN OUR SECONDARY SCHOOL

Helen Floyd

Introduction

I am the lay chaplain in Oaklands Catholic School and Sixth Form College, an academy within the Edith Stein Multi-Academy Trust. We have over 1,400 students from Portsmouth and South East Hampshire. The school mission statement is: 'Community, Unity, Opportunity, No one gets left behind – United by the Cross.' These values define all the activity within the school.

Before becoming a school chaplain, I spent many years as a social worker in many different roles in local authority departments and also in the voluntary sector. I was a team manager in Children's Services, specialising in child protection. I worked with young offenders in mental health teams and in residential and day care services. I then moved into social work training and was a lecturer and course manager in social work and health and social care at Chichester College of Further Education. In different ways, all of these areas of work regularly involved dealing with situations of conflict and broken relationships. I had developed skills and strategies appropriate to these different contexts and found that these were transferable to a secondary school setting. As I developed the reconciliation meeting process at the school, referrals began to come in. Word got round that the meetings were successful, and I found that requests for a reconciliation meeting became increasingly frequent.

Working with the ethos of a Catholic school, within the spiritual dimension of a Christian community, is an important part of our reconciliation process. The reconciliation meetings always take place in the school chapel, where the atmosphere and environment are conducive to peace. The role of chaplain in a faith school lends itself well to this type of work. In our Christian community, reconciliation work is a way in which I can bring the Gospel values of peace, forgiveness and healing to the forefront of my work: 'Blessed are the Peacemakers' (Matthew 5:9, The New Testament). Jesus taught forgiveness, reconciliation and love for everyone, including our enemies.

In this chapter, I describe the 'reconciliation meeting' process in detail. It has been extremely successful as a way of resolving conflicts and bringing peace to relationships between students. I have taught it to staff in other schools and would love to see it used far and wide! At the end of the chapter, I have included a few examples of feedback from students who have experienced the process, and from staff who have referred them.

The negative impact of conflict between students

Throughout my career in education, both as a lecturer in further education, and now in my role of chaplain, I have seen how arguments, fights and broken relationships can be a major cause of unhappiness for students in school and college, and also for staff. They disrupt learning, both for individuals and for groups, reduce focus and concentration during lessons and rapidly spread negative energy among ever larger numbers of individuals and for groups, who then 'take sides' and so fuel the conflict. All this can be hugely stressful and time-consuming for already overstretched staff members to try and sort out. Very often in these situations, parents feel worried and anxious and may become involved by intervening directly in the conflicts, and this can complicate matters further!

There is no doubt that conflict and broken relationships cause deep distress on every level. They can contribute to school refusal, depression, anxiety, eating disorders and other mental health difficulties. The loss of concentration and focus in the classroom can lead to poor academic achievement as well as wasting valuable teaching and learning time if an atmosphere of conflict is present. Hard-working teaching and support staff can find their professional effectiveness significantly constrained by the time and emotional energy needed to deal with the complex and challenging situations that this kind of conflict can produce, and it can be demoralising when efforts to bring about a peaceful resolution are not as effective as hoped.

The role of social media in conflict and bullying has added enormously to the problem. We now see that many humans are capable of writing far more hate-filled comments on a screen than they would ever say to someone face to face. Sadly, and in ways that we do not yet completely understand, the distance, anonymity and, indeed, the power of social media can bring out the worst in many. Unkind comments and outright bullying on social media can cause extreme damage and pain to anyone, especially to the fragile ego of a teenager.

The benefits of reconciliation meetings

When students arrive in the school chapel for a reconciliation meeting, they may be distressed, hurt, angry and deeply troubled. Sometimes, they are visibly burdened by a conflict with another student that has been going on for a very long time. I have found it incredibly rewarding to see them leave 45 minutes later, having made peace with each other, feeling happier, more confident in themselves and with the burden of anger and bitterness lifted.

In most cases, the beneficial results of a reconciliation meeting are immediate and long-lasting. I often ask students for written feedback after their meeting, and I also request this from the staff who referred them. Evaluation and feedback is always an important aspect when introducing any new initiative into an organization, and I have included some examples of these later in this chapter. This helped increase my own confidence that this aspect of my work, all undertaken in the school chapel, has made it possible for a significant contribution to be made to the peaceful running of our large Catholic secondary school.

Why are they called reconciliation meetings?

I feel that the name 'reconciliation meeting' best describes the process I use, and I prefer it to such names as 'conflict resolution' or 'restorative justice'. I believe that reconciliation is far more than simply the resolution of conflict or the restoration of justice, important though both these aims are. Reconciliation is about the healing and repair of broken relationships, about bringing peace where there was once conflict and bitterness and about deepening the awareness and understanding of self and others. Above all, it is about healing and the power of forgiveness in human relationships.

The referral process

The reconciliation meeting can be used for student/student, but may also be used for student/staff or staff/staff situations. Any member of the school community can use the process, although the majority of referrals are for one-to-one student reconciliations. Most referrals come from a head of year, a tutor or a member of the senior leadership team. Students can self-refer and this can be by one or both parties involved in the conflict. Sometimes, a student has been a participant in a previous meeting that has worked successfully for them, and they are keen to repeat the process if difficulties have occurred again with someone else. Or, sometimes, a student has heard from a friend that the meeting in the chapel worked well for them and wants to try it. Clearly, we need to be certain that the self-referral is genuine and not seen as a convenient escape from a lesson, so we always check with the relevant tutor or head of year to ensure that it is a genuine request.

Sometimes, groups of angry, distressed students appear at the door in the midst of a bitter argument and ask: 'Miss, we want to come here and sort it out!' However, although it is good that students see the chapel as a place where they can come for help in sorting out their troubles, I would only agree to their request if it is during their own free time, otherwise the reconciliation could be seen as a good way of getting out of lessons! As a full reconciliation meeting – referred from a member of staff – normally takes place during lesson time, it is important not to bend to pressure. Before agreeing to a self-referral, I will always tell the students that we need to check first with their tutor or head of year. I then explain that if they are in agreement, then a proper appointment will be made for the next day or as soon as possible, and normally only for a one-to-one meeting, not the whole group.

It is my experience that it is usually best to decline requests for a reconciliation meeting for a group of students. Instead, I explain that, at least as a first step, I need to meet with the two main students involved on their own. Problems in relationships nearly always begin with two people and then others get involved as the problem escalates. Young people can be quick to take sides and an unpleasant group rivalry can rapidly develop. It has been my experience that one-to-one reconciliation always works best.

The importance of one-to-ones

A key factor in this process is that, for the main part of all meetings, the two students are left on their own. In one-to-one reconciliation meetings, when the two participants are left on their own, both parties will have a strong feeling of individual responsibility for what happens in the meeting, best described as a sense of ownership of the process. They own the meeting and it is their responsibility alone to make it work. I have found that to have a third party present during conflict resolution, as with any meeting, immediately changes the agenda. It shifts the focus from the two main protagonists involved and introduces a very different dynamic. Part of a student's aim then becomes to impress the third party with their case or to present themselves in a way that encourages others to 'take their side' in the discussion. There may also be things that have happened that either participant may not feel free to discuss in front of a third party but which need to be spoken about at the meeting in order to achieve a full reconciliation.

A request to have a friend to support them during a meeting should always be declined for the same reasons. I usually say to the friend: 'Thank you for supporting your friend by bringing them here, but now you need to go back to class.'

The stages of the reconciliation meeting process

The reconciliation meeting process combines elements of conflict resolution, mediation strategies and interpersonal and listening skills based on open, clear and honest communication. The parties are brought together in a calm, spiritual environment combined with prayer.

It is vital to allow enough time for the different stages of the process to be worked through properly. It is not possible to sort out months of bitter conflict in a few minutes and the meetings will often last for 40 minutes or more, although I firmly believe that an hour should be the maximum time allowed.

There are five stages in the reconciliation meeting. Each one is vital and should be included each time a meeting is held.

Stage One – preparing, welcoming and clarifying the purpose of the meeting and also checking that both participants are motivated to proceed

Stage Two – explaining the guidelines for the meeting

Stage Three – leaving the students on their own to talk and checking their progress every 10 to 15 minutes

Stage Four – talking about dealing with others – demonstration and role play

Stage Five – bringing the meeting to an end, reviewing their learning about themselves and others and then making action plans.

Stage One

It is important to arrange the environment in a way that will be conducive to open, clear and honest communication. Give thought to issues of personal space. Chairs should not be placed too close together as this can feel threatening and uncomfortable. On the other hand, chairs placed too far apart can inhibit effective communication. Do not place chairs at a confrontational angle!

If possible, light a candle for them and also have a peace flag or picture for them to focus on. Ensure that there will not be any interruptions. A calm atmosphere and safe environment are important and these seemingly minor practical issues can make all the difference to the outcome.

Students may arrive separately or together. Do not begin the meeting until both are present. If one arrives first, I greet them, but I then wait in my office until the other arrives. Set a welcoming and positive tone. Check motivation and their aims for the meeting.

The meeting style is that of an open forum. Everything should follow the ideal of open, clear and honest communication. It should be clear that both participants are being treated equally and fairly in a non-judgemental atmosphere.

I start the meeting by thanking the students for coming to the chapel for the meeting and I check that this has been a voluntary decision on their part. The first question I ask separately to each participant, always using their name, is: 'Sam (for example), can you tell me just in one sentence what you would like to get out of this meeting here in the chapel today?' I then repeat the same question to the other student. This helps each one to feel listened to and helps them to clarify their aims. Keep this very brief – one short statement each is enough. It is important that you do not allow students to start telling you all the background details of who did what to whom, although they often want to. Do not let this happen as it does not help your cause and can lead to everyone getting bogged down in details that are not helpful to the process. All you need is a one-sentence overview of what happened and usually this would have already been received from the staff member making the referral.

That first question about their aims is vital. You need to get a constructive answer, something like: 'I want to sort things out' or 'I want these arguments to stop' or 'I want to be friends again.' If the answer is negative: 'I don't know why I'm here' or 'My tutor said I had to come here,' then I do not proceed. I explain that we need more motivation than that to work with or we will not be able to proceed. If one or both are not able to give that, I then send them back to class. This step of checking their motivation is vital. If they do not want to sort things out, then they will not be ready to engage in the process and reconciliation is unlikely to be achieved. Careful observation of body language will help you assess this. If someone appears unmotivated and completely negative, calmly say that you will not go ahead today, but if they change their mind, to let you know and the meeting can be rearranged.

Ask each individual, in turn, to say in one sentence how they are feeling about the situation as it is at present. If they find this question hard to answer, persist with it and try asking it in a different way. It is helpful to get all the negative feelings expressed and out in the open. Their feelings may include anger, betrayal, hurt, confusion and feeling excluded.

At all times, maintain an approach that is positive, calm and affirming in your own tone of voice and your non-verbal communication.

Stage Two

Explain each of the following guidelines carefully. As you do this, ensure that you maintain an even-handed approach, making eye contact to both participants and use their names often. Explain that each guideline needs to be kept to:

- No shouting, pointing or aggressive behaviour of any kind. No intimidation.

- Listen carefully to each other and HEAR what is being said. Listen with the heart. For example, say carefully to one student, making good eye contact, 'Sam, I want you to really listen to John, try and get a better understanding of him and the sort of person he is – try and understand what's going on for him in his life that might be affecting him' (but do not discuss anything that is private or confidential). Then do and say exactly the same to John.

- Ask the students to try and gain an understanding of what went wrong and why. Ask them to be totally honest with each other.

- Tell them to remember that this meeting is not about scoring points, blaming the other or winning the argument, it is about something much more important – about making peace and ending conflict that has been making them both feel so unhappy. It is about each person keeping their dignity and self-respect, and respecting the other – trying to understand each other better and achieve a positive outcome.

- Tell them to make sure that they keep this aim in mind all the time, that they are here to sort things out and achieve reconciliation with each other, to make peace and to leave all the negativity in the past.

- Express confidence and trust: 'I think you can both do this…'

- Remind them how much is at stake – the troubled feelings they have at the moment and that these could all be left behind them today. Remind them that they have the power to change things for the better, no one else will be here, no one else can make them or force them to do it.

Stage Three

I remind them that Jesus is here with them in the chapel and that He always wants to help bring healing into any relationship. I then light a candle and place it on a table in front of them, saying, 'To light you on your way.' I explain that I will now leave them and come back in about 15 minutes to check progress. I tell them that if they are totally stuck then they can ask me for help.

Then I leave them to it! If I had to choose one word to sum up the key to the reconciliation process it would be 'empowerment'. Leaving students on their own, once initial guidelines have been given, is essential to this model of reconciliation. Giving the participants ownership of the process, letting go of any temptation on my part to intervene and handing over control to the participants are important parts of the process.

I have noticed, time and time again, that this kind of letting-go of control is something that many adults find difficult to do because, more often than not, we are used to being in control, especially with younger students, and it can feel alarming to let go. However, it is essential if the process is to work effectively. If you sit in during the meeting, the process will not proceed as it is designed to do. Time and time again, when I ask students: 'Why do you think this meeting worked when other attempts to sort this out have not?' they will answer: 'Because you left us on our own!'

In my work environment, I have the benefit of being able to leave students in the chapel and then returning to my office next door, where I can get on with my work. I leave the door open, and although I cannot hear what they are saying, I can see if they are engaging with each other and would know if anything was happening that would require my intervention. I realise that this is not always possible for everyone, but, ideally, you would be in a separate area, far enough away to give privacy to the meeting but within view of the students and within easy reach if needed. It is vital that the participants have a strong sense that: 'This is our meeting, we are in this on our own.'

Keep your own input brief and resist any temptation to interfere in the process once started. Remember, your job is to empower the young people to do their own work of achieving reconciliation. Exceptions would be if you felt that anyone was at risk of harm, was becoming unduly upset by the process or if they were stuck and not talking at all. I then leave them and return to my office where I pray for them and then get on with other work. Hearing crying or raised voices is not necessarily a reason to intervene! It often happens and needs to be allowed to be worked through. However, where there appears to be considerable distress, your own discretion and judgement must, of course, be used and intervention may be needed. If you are aware that the balance of power is clearly not equal in the relationship, then you may want to be extra cautious and more ready to intervene. If you hear evidence of not sticking to the guidelines, such as shouting or intimidation, then go back and remind them firmly of the rules.

When you go back to check progress after the first 10 or 15 minutes, ask them how they are doing and, unless you get a negative answer, use lots of affirmation and be encouraging. If there is no progress or if they are completely stuck, then you might then sit with them for just a few minutes and maybe help them change the focus or make a constructive suggestion. Keep giving them a sense of ownership of the process: 'This is all up to you.' After giving a brief affirmation, leave again and return to your office. Repeat this every 10 or 15 minutes until the students tell you that they have finished.

Stage Four

When students tell you that a reconciliation has been achieved, then be generous in your praise and affirmation! A second or top-up session should not be needed, except in cases when there is insufficient time to complete the process. It can easily take up to an hour and cannot be rushed. However, often a good reconciliation is achieved in a short time.

Once the actual reconciliation is complete it is vital to deal with the issue of how the participants will each deal with other people who may try to stir things up again when they leave the chapel. It would be only too easy for students, to make a good reconciliation in the chapel, to then lose the progress made by allowing themselves to be influenced by other students, whose agenda is to stir things up again because they have enjoyed the drama of taking sides in the conflict and do not want it to stop. I try and help students to understand that, sadly, a lot of human beings do enjoy watching others fighting and arguing; that's one reason why TV soaps are so popular – they are full of arguments from start to finish!

I always ask them: 'Do you want to be other people's free entertainment?' to which they always answer: 'No!' I then tell them that we will practise a simple technique that they can use, which will enable them to deal with others.

There is a simple strategy that is very effective in dealing with others who try to revisit the argument and engage the participants in further conflict. It is not possible simply to explain it, much better to get the students up and doing it for themselves, so I get them to do a role play that I join in as the third party.

First of all, I ask both students to stand up. Then, I invite one student to role play what she/he would do if someone comes up and tries to restart the conflict. Taking the third party role, I then go up to them and say something like: 'Hey, Emma, do you know what I just heard Jess saying about you? She was really horrible about you, you should go and sort her out!' Usually, that gets their attention and they start to listen. I then point out that once they start listening to this sort of thing, their curiosity will get the better of them and they will fall straight into the trap! What they need is a quick and effective strategy to put into practice immediately when they are in that situation. We then reverse roles, where I play the student and get them to play the third party and say the same thing to me. I then demonstrate the technique as follows:

- Instantly give the STOP sign, hand held politely but firmly up in front of you.

- Make positive eye contact, smile confidently, use confident body language.

- Make one, clear, positive statement: 'We've sorted it all out now, thank you.'

- Walk briskly and confidently away.

- Do not turn round, whatever else they may say to you, just keep walking.

Practice this with each student, in turn, until they can do it with confidence! Sometimes, a student will change the words that they have been asked to say, but insist that they stick to that one clear positive statement, delivered with confidence. The STOP sign must be given immediately. Explain that if they start listening, then it will not work.

A great benefit of role playing in this way is that it invariably makes everyone laugh and that is a great antidote to the tension that has been present earlier in the meeting.

Stage Five

I bring the reconciliation meeting to an end. If reconciliation has been achieved, then I affirm and praise the students (sometimes, a second session may be needed). I also help the students to think about what they have learned about themselves and each other during the process of reconciliation. They make notes of how they felt and how things were before and after the meeting. They finish by making action plans for the future of their relationship.

Conclusion

I recommend this model of reconciliation as an effective contribution to achieving peace in school. It can and does make a real difference. It can be used by anyone so long as each step of the process, as set out above, is adhered to rigorously. It is as much a question of what you do not do, as what you do do! Remember at all times that the key principle is empowerment, making it clear to the participants that the responsibility for the outcome of their meeting is on them.

It is unusual for a reconciliation meeting not to produce a successful result, but it can happen. This may be due to more complex mental health or behavioural issues than such a meeting is able to address. However, do not be deterred from continuing to use it. Your confidence in the reconciliation process is an important factor in itself and will always communicate itself to the participants. On one occasion after a long and tearful meeting, a student was simply not able to forgive the other for the deep hurt caused. Of course, forgiveness is not always instant, it can take time. I invited her to sit in front of the cross in the chapel and take some time to reflect and pray on her own. I made an appointment with them for the next day, saying that they should only come back if they wanted to continue the meeting. They both came back and a full reconciliation was achieved.

Have confidence in the process! There have sometimes been occasions when students have come into the chapel in such a hostile state that I have thought to myself: 'This one's never going to work!'

– but they do! I have run training workshops for other chaplains and it is always so good to receive positive feedback that the process has produced positive results in their schools.

Finally, I include some examples of feedback from students and staff that I hope will give a flavour of how reconciliation has been helpful to them.

Examples of feedback from students

I often ask students to do brief written feedback at the end of the meeting, saying in their own words why they think that the meeting was successful, how they feel now and what they have learned about themselves. Here are some typical examples that help to give a sense of how the process works:

> I think it worked in the chapel because no one interrogated us in a way that we feel forced. It was a nice calm place in the chapel and it felt like we could be honest also we didn't have a teacher to interrupt and so we didn't need to be worried about saying some things we wanted to say… When I came in here I was sad and felt betrayed now I feel like a weight has been lifted off my shoulders and I feel happy. I think I have learned that I tend to overreact to stuff and I get stressed easily. I will think about that in future. (Girl in Year 9)

> I think that I have found out that I take things too far. More than I need to sometimes. It worked well in the chapel because no one was there and it was just me and her and no one else… When I came in I felt angry and uptight, now I feel like I did the right thing coming to the chapel as I feel much better and we are friends again. (Girl in Year 8)

> We had been fighting every day since Year 4 in primary school, every day something bad happened, our teachers and parents tried to sort it out but it didn't work. It carried on into this school, I used to hate coming into school sometimes I told my mum I wasn't going. But now we have had this meeting in the chapel it has worked, we sorted ourselves out and we made a plan to stop the arguments and fights. I feel much better that we went and it resolved everything, I'm much better in lessons now. We are not friends, but we keep peace with each other. I have learned that you can keep bad things going even if you

don't really want to, but I know now there is a way to stop. (Boy in Year 8, interviewed six weeks after the reconciliation meeting)

I felt sad, lonely and disappointed, I had no one to hang around with, there was something missing inside of me, I wanted to say sorry to people I'd been mean to, but I couldn't do it and some friends did not help this problem. After this chapel reconciliation I feel so much better now it is all solved, Jesus helped us to make peace and say sorry and forgive each other, no one interfered, we did the meeting ourselves, I feel much happier. (Girl in Year 7)

We came into the chapel feeling really angry at each other, which had been going on for ages. We constantly had arguments I couldn't stand it. I couldn't concentrate on anything at school. But with the help in the chapel we spoke about everything alone, we talked about what was bothering us and why. We made a promise to stop arguing and told each other what had made us upset. Now we are best friends again so I feel a lot better, my mum will be pleased. (Girl in Year 7)

After I came to the chapel I feel relieved and light. When I came in I felt like there was a big burden on my shoulders. Now I feel very relaxed and I feel like the argument has stopped for sure. I am going to live more happily and positively. I have learned that I am weak in some ways but I can be strong, depending on the situation. (Boy in Year 8)

In the time I've spent in the chapel I now feel disappointed with myself. I now understand that S was very upset by what was happening, I did not realise that before. I see now I shouldn't have let things get the better of me, but I had stuff going on in my family that were getting me down. I have told S my story and how I feel and how sorry I am and now she has forgiven me so it is a big relief. I have learned that I have never had the experience of knowing how to say positive, kind things to people. (Girl in Year 8, a referral due to serious bullying)

I learned that you shouldn't always listen to people because they might not be telling you the truth, just trying to wind you up. I think it worked here in the chapel because we were alone and nobody was here to stop us or interrupt or distract us. I would use this again if it happened with someone else. (Boy in Year 9)

Before I came here I felt bad and I wanted to cry, through this process I feel relieved now as we have sorted this out and I feel like I am a better person in life. I hope that this change will last a long time. Reconciliation was not as hard as I expected and I have learned more about the other person. (Boy in Year 9)

At first I was really sad and annoyed at this other girl and I could not even look at her, but now I think we can become friends quite quickly again. Now I can look at her and I can definitely say that going to the chapel worked. I feel happy now. It worked because I got to talk to her in peace and quiet so no one else got to listen to the conversation. (Girl in Year 10)

Examples of feedback from staff members

As a member of staff I think that the reconciliation work is really important to us as a school. When students fall out it can often involve a number of different students and sometimes different friendship groups. In a school environment a lot of students are in close proximity to each other, and arguments and bad feelings can be fuelled by students not being able to get away from each other, as well as other students getting involved or taking sides. Social media can also really inflame problems. When this happens I have found it difficult to find time and space to get the students together quickly enough. It is also sometimes very difficult to know where to start in getting students to talk to each other and move forward. One thing I have noticed about reconciliation in the chapel is that students who are unwilling to talk to staff about their issues, and who will point blank refuse to engage with each other, will be surprisingly willing to go to the chapel and sit down. I am also often surprised at how quickly the students move from anger, bitterness and hurt to calmness and acceptance. As a teacher and form tutor it is very reassuring to know that I have the option of referring students to talk to the chaplain and each other. I know that there are effective options when I do not have the right words or enough time to help students move forward from anger, distrust and deep hurt. (A Year 9 tutor)

The benefit of mediation and restorative justice is tangible within a school community when it is done well. To see two upset, sometimes angry, often hurt, young people come together in a sacred space to listen and talk and heal is a powerful experience. To watch and listen as they cry, laugh, hug and then pray together is a privilege because they do it with hearts and spirits lifted from the gloom of damaged friendships into the light of a real relationship. In an age when young people use social media to communicate, the power of eye-to-eye, face-to-face contact – looking at someone and saying sorry, accepting an apology from someone else – is something they rarely experience which is why it is ever more important we foster it in our schools because we know that it heals and restores them. In turn, that nurtures our community; it dispels the bitterness and hardness of heart as forgiveness and compassion once again become a reality within our school. The gift of a mediator, a chaplain, in school is a precious blessing whose value cannot be overstated. (A senior leadership team member)

Helen has made a huge impact on the pastoral welfare of my year group. She has worked regularly to help students reconcile, and she facilitates this in a way that empowers the students and provides them with skills that they can take with them and use again. The key to this is in allowing the students to have a suitable environment to discuss their issues or concerns and making sure that they have agreed ground rules before they start. After this Helen withdraws, leaving the students to have their own private discussion, so she is very much in the background to guide and support them through the process. Her deep faith is very much evident and so students feel they can open up to her and share worries as they see her as someone that they can trust and who can guide them also in a spiritual way. (A head of year)

CHAPTER 6

A PEACEFUL CLASSROOM
CREATING SPACE AND USING PHILOSOPHY FOR CHILDREN

Christine Easom

Introduction

I have been involved in the Peaceful Schools Movement right from the start with the founder Anna Lubelska. We used to talk about the need for a book about peaceful schools and so I was very excited to hear that Jessica Kingsley Publishers was going to make this happen! In my chapter, I share my journey of creating a peaceful classroom and pupils' thoughts and ideas about peaceful schools that I gathered during my research for the Peaceful Schools Movement.

I studied to become a teacher at Bishop Grosseteste College in Lincoln. Originally from South London, I have lived and worked in Staffordshire since 1980. I was Head of Religious Education at a Specialist Humanities College until 2009 and have since worked independently, offering introductory training and workshops with Philosophy for Children (P4C) and creative approaches to Religious Education.

A journey from fear to freedom

When I was seven years old, my teacher told me to stand in the rubbish bin at the front of the class because, in her words, that was where I belonged. I have no idea what I had done or how many minutes I stood there, staring at the blackboard, feeling humiliation and anger rise from my feet to my tummy and to my face, but it felt like forever. I felt a sense of injustice, but it was overwhelmed by a belief that adults knew best and that other people must be right. I must be a child of a lesser kind, if not actually rubbish. Ten years later, I was an A-level student, confidently enjoying learning. I had found subjects that I loved and was fortunate to have several teachers who grew our self-confidence. Somewhere between these two experiences I decided to be a teacher. The first experience convinced me that there must be a better way to treat children and help them learn. The second proved it to be true.

For 35 years, I studied and taught Religious Education in middle and secondary schools. The nature of the subject meant that I was constantly looking for and finding content and methods that could cultivate an atmosphere conducive to the best kind of learning. My school experiences as well as my training convinced me that the best learning happens when children feel comfortable, accepted, safe, confident and motivated. These simple conditions seem obvious but the pressures of our education system, while assenting to these aims, create conditions that mitigate against them.

It is a courageous school community with imaginative staff who take on the challenge of meeting the requirements of the system while acknowledging the rights of the students as human beings and giving them the space to discover what that means. As a teacher, I took responsibility for the atmosphere generated in the classroom. I understood that I was the trained, paid professional who chose to be in this position. I accepted that it was up to me to create a space where students could learn the requirements of my subject but, more importantly, learn as and to be individual human beings, growing in self-confidence and the skills to lead full lives.

I reflected on my preparation and organisation of lessons, constantly reviewing what had gone well and what could be improved. I addressed difficulties in discipline by asking myself what I could do differently and examining the personal insecurities that drove me to impatience or misjudgement. I set respect for the students as my top priority, believing that by example, the classroom would become a space where all individuals would grow in respect for themselves, for one another and for learning.

One day, about eight years into my career, I was standing in my classroom with happy, active, respectful young people working peacefully together, and I realised that I was teaching in the way I had always wanted to. It was possible and it had happened and it felt wonderful.

In my desire to teach well, I had stumbled upon a recipe for creating a peaceful space. It was a space where young people could talk, share and listen without fear of judgement or humiliation and they were happy doing it. Students walked into my classroom and said that it was peaceful and exciting. Other teachers would come in to ask something and comment that everyone was working peacefully or that the space was very tranquil. One student asked if she could live in my classroom because it was always so calm and peaceful.

A creative space

As a young teacher, I was at first ill-equipped for the job and I learned from watching others, imitating the best and avoiding the pitfalls of the worst. I learned that it is easy to get caught up in petty disagreements with students and that having a calm, controlled start to a lesson was essential. I learned that organisation was key. If I was confident, calm and clear at the start of the lesson, students would settle quickly, assured that they could understand and meet the expectations of the lesson.

At the start of working with a new class, we discussed and agreed on the ground rules for the year ahead. We talked about what made a lesson work well and what stopped that from happening. The students talked about the content of lessons, the behaviour of other students and the attitude of the teacher. They would usually raise all of the issues that were important to address and the chance to air their worries and hear from others usually resulted in a degree of trust that immediately impacted the quality of relationships and learning in a positive way.

The students recorded the agreed rules on the front page of their notebooks and there were opportunities for them to be reviewed, added to or changed. Opening up issues that impact the teacher and the learners in a trusting and tolerant way shows that this is an honest space and one in which it is OK to address common difficulties fearlessly in order to make the learning better for everyone.

My teacher training emphasised the creation of a stimulating and flexible classroom. I trained to teach in middle schools, and the college had a special interest in integrated teaching in primary schools. I learned to see the classroom as a space that could be physically organised differently from day to day or even lesson to lesson. We moved desks around, often placing them against the walls, with the students sitting in a circle and only turning to their desks when there was a need to write. The walls were used to record work in progress, display pupils' work, share ideas from class to class, pose thought-provoking questions and stimulate responses through bold and colourful images. The displays were frequently changed and students took responsibility for choosing themes to illustrate and designing the materials.

The important thing was that the space was active and alive. This produced a sense of expectation in the students, who would regularly arrive at the door excited about what we were doing on a given day and what the room would be like. I often played music as students came into the classroom. It might be a song or instrumental that had a connection with the theme of the lesson, or a sound that was intriguing or calming. Sometimes, they didn't realise that there was music playing as they moved from a busy, noisy corridor into the classroom. As the students got ready for the lesson, they would hear the music and as it drew their attention and curiosity, they listened attentively, settling down without the need for me to talk or instruct or appeal for quiet. This simple strategy created an identity for the classroom and an impact for the lesson.

However, a peaceful classroom is much more than simply a space where students settle well to learn and where the relationships are harmonious more often than not. A peaceful classroom must prove its worth through the way in which moments of conflict are addressed and tested by the attitudes and skills that students develop to understand and deal with conflict in life. Conflict is a natural and necessary experience. Disagreement is not something to avoid at all costs. Reason and argument are vital tools in the process of understanding the nature of conflict. Hearing people's stories and experiences helps us to empathise and appreciate the differences that make us who we are.

Much of the school day is prescriptive and about fulfilling set objectives with little space to sit with uncertainty or tension. Subsequently, difficult issues are often brushed under the carpet or taken in hand by a member of staff in a punitive manner. This is always unsatisfactory and leads to further conflict. A peaceful classroom is one that creates ways to open up difficulties, addressing them with patience, confidence, resilience and respect for the needs of all.

Looking for meaning

In Daniel H. Pink's (2008) book *A Whole New Mind*, he looks at the nature and power of creative thinking and explores this under the six headings: Design, Story, Symphony, Empathy, Play and Meaning. These chapters look at the development of a more sensory approach to learning. Pink begins his chapter on meaning with reference to an Austrian Jew named Viktor Frankl. A young psychiatrist, Frankl was rounded up by the authorities in 1942 and later taken to Auschwitz. He had been working on a manuscript of his theories and his wife, Tilly, sewed it into the lining of his coat to be preserved. After the SS guards took his coat from him, he spent the next three years scratching his theories onto scraps of paper. However, this time, he had his experiences of the horrors of captivity as a testing ground and illustration of his ideas.

After his liberation, Frankl published his theories and reflections in a book, *Man's Search for Meaning*. This narrative is not an easy read. It describes the reality of cruel imprisonment and the fight for survival. It documents the phases that the human body, mind and spirit pass through as a person attempts to live in such conditions. Frankl comes to the conclusion that those who find meaning in their experiences have the greatest chance of survival.

Frankl observed and experienced for himself how small moments of meaningful encounter or reflection could sustain a person through unimaginable horrors. He saw how meaning can be found in suffering and how people driven by a search for meaning can find strength, even in the most terrible of circumstances. This made sense to me as a teacher.

In the classroom, I witnessed how young learners were stimulated by a sense of purpose in learning. If they found the lesson meaningful, they found it interesting and their interest would drive their energy, commitment, resilience, determination and creativity. These factors had a far greater effect on learning than rewards or punishments. The glorious challenge for the teacher is to find ways of making the learning of their subject meaningful. This takes courage, desire, time and willingness to change tack when necessary. It may mean challenging the teacher's own assumptions and it will mean taking the needs and opinions of the students seriously. In a peaceful classroom, that sense of meaning and purpose will draw disparate personalities together as individuals learn about each other, hear one another's stories and build a community that is creative and purposeful.

A space to choose

While reading *Man's Search for Meaning*, I happened upon the following by Viktor Fankl: 'Between stimulus and response there is a space. In that space is our power to choose our response. In our response lies our growth and our freedom.' This made sense to me, in part because I had been using stilling and meditation in the classroom for many years and I realised that there was value in moments of quiet space in lessons. Also, I had been using and training in Philosophy for Children (P4C) and I was beginning to understand the nature and effect of philosophical space.

Teaching and learning involve a constant stream of stimuli. From the start of each day, there are instructions, expectations, requests, and demands. To every stimulus there is an individual response and among groups of individuals there are many different responses. The potential for misunderstanding and misjudgement is enormous. Many of the habits of teaching and learning are rooted in an immediate and habitual response to things that we think we know yet fail to observe carefully or afresh. As teachers, learners and human beings, we often respond on autopilot, without allowing time to challenge our impulses and subsequent behaviours.

The above quotation from Frankl made me look again and again at my own capacity for allowing myself to be in the space between stimulus and response. I realised that I do not have to respond immediately. I began to recognise the habits that led my immediate responses and I questioned them. I recognised the assumptions that would immediately come into play and I began to let them go. What opened up was a creative space, where I discovered a freedom to choose an alternative response – one that was more measured, truthful and creative.

A peaceful classroom is one where those with power and authority are able to create space. That space should allow individuals to speak freely, think creatively and reflect honestly. That thinking and reflection should, in turn, enable individuals to make reasonable, creative choices that impact positively on themselves and others. In such a space, the opportunities for growth are endless and the growth is one towards liberation. Such growth, I believe, is at the heart of peaceful relationships. Such relationships enable conflict to be transformed from something that destroys and undermines, into a vehicle for understanding and learning from difference in all its richness.

A questioning space and the use of P4C

As a teacher of Religious Studies, questions and questioning were naturally at the heart of my teaching and learning. Asking simple questions with many possible responses generated conversations that students found interesting and stimulating. I recall a Year 7 lesson about the existence and nature of God which, when interrupted by the dinner-time bell, caused a student to call out, 'We can't go now because this is possibly the most important discussion we will ever have!'

Whilst not every pupil was always engaged to the same extent, questions, conversation and listening generated an atmosphere of openness. That openness to possibilities and valuing individual pupils' experiences and opinions gave the learning an integrity that was respected. Students who were not altogether interested in a specific topic became interested in the thoughts of other people and encouraged by the opportunity to express and consider alternative points of view. The classroom was at times a forum for heated debate and at other times one of thoughtful reflection. It was noticeable that as students opened up and shared their personal experiences, other students followed suit and their capacity to understand and empathise with each other grew.

P4C is one way of using questioning in the classroom. I was introduced to it through training offered by Will Ord. I remember attending his workshop in Staffordshire and feeling that I had rediscovered some humanity in learning. Not only was the training accessible and implementable, but it also offered a way of learning that valued people most of all. P4C is a pedagogy that began with the work of Professor Matthew Lipman, who founded the Institute for the Advancement of Philosophy for Children at Montclair State University in New Jersey, USA, in 1974. Inspired by ideas in philosophical and scientific enquiry, he believed that young children had the capability to think rationally and could be encouraged to think philosophically. Today, Philosophy for Children is practiced in more than 60 countries around the world, and, in the UK, it is especially promoted and supported by the Society for Advancing Philosophical Enquiry and Reflection in Education (SAPERE).

The community of enquiry

At the heart of P4C is the 'community of enquiry'. The community of enquiry is a group of people of any age, who together enquire into a question or idea, searching for understanding and seeking truth. During an enquiry, a stimulus, such as a story, an image, a short video, a poem or an object, is presented to the community. The community has time to think and talk about the stimulus and their responses to it. Philosophical questions are then created in response to the conversation. The community then talks about a question chosen by the community. In a community of enquiry, participants sit in a circle so that they look to, and learn with and from, each other. The teacher becomes a facilitator, someone who guides the community through the enquiry process. Their role is to encourage the community to notice, question and reflect on their own thinking. As the community grows in confidence, it also develops a sense of shared responsibility for the conversation and behaviours. The space to reflect and review grows naturally through the enquiry process.

People can share personal experiences to support their views and, as they do so, the community learns to understand and care for others. With time, the conversation and the activity of the community becomes:

- Collaborative – as people work together in thinking and decision-making

- Creative – as they build on the ideas of others, make connections, take risks in their thoughts and words and offer imaginative responses

- Critical – as ideas are challenged, reasoned arguments are used and people are willing to change their mind

- Caring – as individuals become aware of and consider the feelings, experiences and needs of the people in the community. They also come to care about the quality, value and integrity of the thinking.

The process of a P4C enquiry

Warm up/preparation

This is a short space to calm down, focus and improve participants' awareness of each other. Use games that will get students mixing and talking, or activities that will focus concentration.

Agreeing ground rules

The community agrees some basic guidelines, which will secure a full and fair experience for everyone. This may not be appropriate before every enquiry and the community can choose to review, change or dispose of them if they are no longer helpful.

Presentation/stimulus

A story, picture, poem, object or other stimulus is presented to the community. Choose something that will stimulate lots of ideas and that is topical, relevant and exciting to the eye and mind.

Thinking time/reflection

This is space for individuals to think and respond to the stimulus. Ask participants to gather their first thoughts and questions on paper or just in their mind.

Conversation/sharing

This is a space to share private responses in twos or threes. Ask the students to share their thoughts and questions in small groups.

Formulation

As individuals or in small groups, people create philosophical questions that arise from the conversation. Ask the groups to compose their own question/s, arising from their thinking, and present their ideas as a philosophical question.

Airing

Questions are shared with the community and the ideas clarified if necessary. During this stage, any connections between the questions can be noted and questions can be combined if the same one arises several times from different groups. Ask one person from each group to share the question with the community.

Selection/voting

The community chooses the question that they want to talk about. Ask the community to vote for the question that they want to talk about. Voting methods could include: vote for only one question, vote for as many questions as you like, vote with eyes closed or vote by standing next to the question you like.

First words

In pairs or groups, individuals share their initial thoughts about the question chosen. Ask those who created the chosen question to comment and share their views to begin the shared dialogue.

Building

This is the heart of the dialogue as the members of the community build on each other's ideas and open up lines of enquiry. As the community talks together, they search for possible answers to their question.

Last words

Everyone is invited to share a last thought about the question and the enquiry. Go around the circle, asking for a volunteer to start and allow people to pass if they do not want to contribute.

Review

This is an opportunity to reflect on how the session went and what the community has learned together. Ask students what they think worked well and what they would do differently next time.

As I used P4C I saw that it offered an approach to teaching and learning that was academically stimulating and meaningful, while being liberating for both individuals and communities. It has the potential to bring down walls between people and in their own thinking. It challenges individuals to face their own ideas and habits of mind. P4C opens up space where there is a freedom to sit with uncertainty, imagine different responses, test ideas and make informed choices. The students I taught enjoyed P4C. They enjoyed the space to talk and think without judgement from a teacher. They enjoyed working with others and they came to understand one another more fully. They enjoyed the affirmation from their peers but also the challenges presented by arguing with them. Shy students gained confidence and confident students learned to listen to others. It is impossible in a few paragraphs to do justice to the enormity of the benefits offered by P4C. It is something that you just have to try.

With the power of P4C in mind, I was interested to see how it could enable students to think and talk about Peaceful Schools. I was interested in their thoughts and questions on the topic and how they would assess P4C as a process that could contribute to people and communities being or becoming peaceful.

The Staffordshire schools enquiries into peace and peaceful schools

During 2011 and 2012, I worked with a small number of students from schools in Staffordshire to enquire into the idea of 'Peaceful Schools'. The students were from Years 5, 7, 10 and 13. I would like to thank the pupils and staff at Wolstanton High School Newcastle, Richard Wakefield C of E Primary School Tutbury and the Staffordshire Student SACRE (Standing Advisory Council for Religious Education) for their participation in the sessions outlined.

What follows is a snapshot of some of the questions, ideas and conclusions that emerged from enquiries. I was interested in their views on school as a peaceful place, if schools can be peaceful places and how schools might become peaceful places. I also asked them to assess whether the community of enquiry can help schools to be peaceful places.

I hope that teachers and others working with young people will find some inspiration in the questions, responses and conclusions presented in this work. For those who took part, the experience of working with P4C to ask questions about peaceful schools allowed them to share their fears and anxieties about being at school as well as their hopes for their own education and that of others. It showed us all that asking philosophical questions in the community of enquiry opens up ideas and values individual experiences. It showed us that through enquiry, everyone's assumptions and expectations could be challenged, therefore allowing something new, unexpected and exciting to emerge.

No definition of peace or peacefulness was given to the students. Any definitions of peace or peacefulness, and ideas about the nature and value of peace or peacefulness, were generated and explored through the enquiry process. Any assumptions about the nature and value of peace and peacefulness and about peaceful schools were explored as they arose through the dialogue. The sessions followed the concerns and questions that arose among the students in response to the stimulus presented. In the final session, the pupils assessed P4C as a process that could help to build the attitudes and relationships that might help a school to become a peaceful place. Some of the pupils had experience of using P4C but most of them had not used P4C before.

Some of the things that pupils in Years 5, 6 and 7 associated with peaceful places

Nature

Seeing something different

Being with/thinking about people I love

Being free to do what I want

Being quiet

Feeling my cat breathe on my face

Being alone and no one can be mean to me

There is calm music playing

Playing a game

There are no distractions/No one can bother me

It can feel calm, even when there is a lot of noise around

It is big and there is a lot of room to think

I have a friend that I feel peaceful with

The beach – because there are things to explore

Being safe

Family meals

Not being judged

I shut the door and I am by myself

Where I can think about my thoughts

Where I can sit and do something in my own time

Where you can wipe the slate clean and start a new life

Just me and my thoughts

Questions created by the students

Questions about peace

What is peace like?

Is there any such thing as peace?

Is peace a good thing?

Questions about peacefulness

To be peaceful do you need friends?

Do you have to feel comfortable and relaxed to be peaceful?

What is peaceful?

Do you think this is peaceful?

Questions about peaceful places

What are peaceful places like?

Where is my peaceful place?

Why is my peaceful place like this?

Is it always quiet in a peaceful place?

Are peaceful places possible?

What is a peaceful place?

Are peaceful places happy places?

Can peaceful places be noisy places?

Questions about peaceful schools

Is school a peaceful place?

Why would you want a peaceful school?

What would a peaceful school be like?

Is it possible for school to be peaceful?

Would a peaceful school be boring?

Why isn't school peaceful?

Would everyone be happy in a peaceful school?

If we made a peaceful school, would it make people happy?

What would make a school peaceful?

What would a peaceful subject be?

Questions chosen by the students for enquiry

Do you feel peaceful in a peaceful place?

What is possible in my peaceful place?

Who is in charge in a peaceful school?

Is a peaceful school a place where you don't get judged by your appearance or personality?

Can you ever feel completely safe?

Would being peaceful make us better learners or people?

Year 5 pupils talking about peaceful places and feeling peaceful

> Places can feel peaceful or not peaceful, depending on how you feel inside.

> You can feel peaceful anywhere if you feel peaceful inside.

> Some places feel different to different people.

> It depends what mood you are in and what has happened to you.

> A peaceful place could feel scary.

Year 5 pupils talking about what a peaceful school would be like

The students said that safety is important because, if you don't feel safe, then you can't relax and enjoy being at school. They said that people running down the corridors and pushing into people could be an example of not being safe. One girl suggested that 'being friends' was most important because, if people were friendly with each other, then they would be careful and look out for one another. She suggested that this would mean that people wouldn't hurt one anther or would help if someone did get hurt.

A boy suggested that 'being accepted' was the most important thing because if people accepted one another, then they would be friends and have more friends. It would also mean that people would be less likely to hurt one another accidentally.

Another girl said that if people were more able to do this, then they might 'find something inside themselves that they didn't know was there'.

One boy said that in a peaceful classroom, the teacher would be more able to notice when children were being mean to one another because it would be quieter.

Three girls discussed how a school that was too peaceful might be boring and that people would not be acting normally! They acted out two scenarios with a teacher and pupils interacting in a way that was peaceful but artificial and a way that was disrespectful but honest. They said that a really peaceful school would be somewhere between these two examples.

Two boys drew and commented on a picture of positive things that would be visible in the school. These included people learning happily, having fun, teachers and pupils laughing together and people helping one another. They thought that such a school would have older pupils helping younger pupils. Three girls performed a drama sketch, showing how students might help one another when they were hurt. This showed the pupils forgiving one another and the teacher showing acceptance. They said that a teacher could show the students how to be accepting and forgiving.

Some questions raised about peaceful schools by Year 7 students

How do different subjects encourage peace or peaceful atmospheres?

What is the relationship between happiness and peace?

What do we mean by happiness at school? Is it different from outside school?

Is a peaceful school where you don't get judged by your appearance or personality?

Is it possible for everyone to have their needs and wants met at school?

Would there be winners and losers in a peaceful school?

What is the relationship between being peaceful and learning?

What is the relationship between being peaceful and being a human being?

A Year 7 enquiry into what makes a school peaceful

This is the question they chose to discuss: 'Is a peaceful school where you don't get judged by your appearance or personality?' The dialogue focused on the following ideas:

If you don't judge, then you don't know who to be friends with.

Everyone judges others, but you don't have to do it in a negative way.

You shouldn't judge on the basis of what others say.

You should find out things for yourself before you make a judgement about others.

You need to judge others in order to be safe.

It is human nature to judge others on their appearance and personality.

Everyone does it, but not everyone admits to it.

You are judged all the time at school because there is a lot of competition.

The Year 7 enquiry was followed up with an active learning lesson that used drama and role play to explore questions around safety in school. The students identified relationships with teachers and other students as the main focus of their feelings and experiences of being safe or unsafe. Some students said that it was easier and more effective to work through their feelings of being unsafe by doing role play. Some students said that the community of enquiry was a good place to share their feelings and questions about being unsafe. They said that if students talked together like this more often, they would learn to trust each other. They said that teachers should be participants in the enquiry and then they could understand what it felt like for the students.

Student thoughts on whether the community of enquiry can help to build a peaceful school

- It helps people to work together in a calm way.

- We learned to take turns, show respect and listen to other opinions.

- We supported and encouraged each other.

- We were able to talk about difficult things.

- Listening carefully to others.

- Being able to explain what we mean without rushing.

- It helped people to make friends.

- It could make people more confident.

- It let you speak.

- Knowing that people have their own opinions.

- Learning to be a peaceful class.

- Knowing that we could talk about difficult things without anyone laughing at us or telling us we were wrong.

- It made me feel like I was as important as everyone else.

- I thought about things I have never thought about before.

- I learned to not be afraid of saying my thoughts and opinions.

- It was really nice to be able to work calmly and quietly with people listening to each other.

My thoughts on how the community of enquiry might contribute to the building of a peaceful school

It helps individuals to:

- listen to and learn to appreciate the experiences, thoughts, feelings and perspectives of others

- offer their thoughts, experiences, feelings and views

- develop appreciation of a range of different experiences

- learn how to challenge and trust themselves, others and the thinking process

- challenge their own and other people's expectations and assumptions in a supportive community

- talk about issues, questions and experiences to do with power, control, equality and fairness

- learn to talk about difficult, controversial, challenging and uncomfortable ideas in a supportive environment

- develop understanding and appreciation of differences between people as well as the things that people have in common

- talk openly about the things that matter to them

- explore what it means to be in a safe space with others

- build relationships with others that are based on trust and equality

- learn to sit with uncertainty and non-judgement

- develop confidence in themselves and others

- participate in dialogue and activity that is meaningful and relevant to specific circumstances and experiences

- be willing to change their opinions in the light of discussion and evidence

- engage in thinking that can have a radical and practical impact on individuals and organisations.

Concluding thoughts

I believe that Philosophy for Children (P4C) can be used to stimulate thinking and discussion about peaceful classrooms and it can contribute to the building of peaceful schools. Young learners who become philosophical become attentive, observant and reasonable. They learn to think about their thinking and become open to changing their minds willingly. The atmosphere generated by enquiry spills over into other aspects of school life as young learners grow in confidence and self-efficacy. The challenge for the school becomes one of listening to and learning with and from their students.

I hope to encourage teachers, and others working with young people, to consider embracing the P4C approach as a route to challenging, meaningful and purposeful dialogue that leads to real and lasting change that affects individuals and communities.

Throughout my years of teaching, and, indeed, throughout my own education, I was convinced that classrooms should and could be places where individuals of different ages and persuasions could learn peacefully together. This is not easy in a climate of competition and accountability, where time is at a premium and the space to reflect is squeezed. It presents challenges to the curriculum, organisation and attitudes to authority. However, I have seen it transform young people's attitudes to learning and to one another. I have loved and felt honoured to be part of a movement in education that challenges students to be alongside one another, listening to each other, thinking about thinking and changing their thoughts and actions because they have heard other people's stories and have cared.

Further reading

Erricker, C. and Erricker, J. (eds) (2001) *Meditation in Schools*. London and New York: Continuum.

Frankl, V. (1959) *Man's Search for Meaning*. London: Rider.

Haynes, J. (2008) *Children as Philosophers: Learning through Enquiry and Dialogue in the Primary Classroom*. London: Routledge.

Lantieri, L. (2008) *Building Emotional Intelligence*. Boulder, CO: Sounds True.

Lewis, L. (ed.) (2012) *Philosophy for Children through the Secondary Curriculum*. London: Continuum.

Pink, D.H. (2008) *A Whole New Mind*. London: Marshall Cavendish.

Stone, M. (1995) *Don't Just Do Something, Sit There: Developing Children's Spiritual Awareness*. Norwich: Religious and Moral Press.

Organisations and websites

For further information about resources used in the peaceful schools research work, contact Christine Easom on creativespaceseducation@hotmail.co.uk

For information on using and training in Philosophy for Children, contact: www.sapere.org.uk and www.thinkingeducation.co.uk.

CHAPTER 7

THE IMPORTANCE OF SCHOOL GROUNDS

Felicity Robinson

Introduction

Children grow in confidence and learn new skills outdoors. Some positively blossom when they are beyond the confines of the classroom walls, seeing the relevance of the core curriculum in the world outside. This is what motivates me to work with schools.

I am a teacher and landscape architect, specialising in the use and development of school grounds. Over the years, I have discovered that school grounds can have a vital role in the creation of a peaceful environment and culture within any school. The fact is that well-managed and well-used grounds make a very positive contribution to peaceful schools.

In this chapter, I look at why and how learning, play and recreation outside in the grounds is important and valued in many schools. I also offer you an audit checklist of points to consider when looking at your own school grounds.

Schools are often tight for space – you can't find breakout spots, classrooms may be cramped and stuffy and Year 6s are working in rooms better suited to Key Stage 1 children. Are these familiar to you in some primary schools? Secondary schools and Early Years settings can have similar issues and the reflections in this chapter are equally relevant to all phases.

Now, imagine children working in spacious environments and airy conditions, where noise is not an issue. Imagine a school where there are a variety of places of different character offering space for quiet breakout work or large group collaborative activities. A school with spaces where large-scale, energetic, wet, messy science and art are easy to organise, and engaged on-task children can be seen enjoying their learning. This is the potential of your school grounds – large or small, urban or rural!

Weather? Yes, of course this is an issue, but well-designed multi-functional places can be used in all four seasons so as to enrich curriculum delivery. The right clothing helps, too!

Some of you may be lucky enough to have brilliant buildings but you will also know that the external spaces can offer complementary learning environments. Indeed, there are some elements of the curriculum that can only be taught effectively outdoors, often in science but also in other core subjects, where first-hand experience teaches more than any paper-based task or online animation can do.

Playtime and breaktime use of the grounds and sports provision are of course key functions, and this chapter will look at grounds for play and recreation as well as learning.

The benefits of learning outdoors

My starting point is to see children as learners and to find out what interests and motivates them to learn and how to engage them. This can be a key to their greater attainment. From observations, we can learn a lot from their playtimes during which they are, by and large, intrinsically motivated to cooperate, to negotiate and to be creative thinkers. However, this does not happen readily in bland, monotonous spaces. Children frequently use any found objects or incidental spaces for creative play such as stones, weeds, steps, rails, etc. A checklist of ideas to audit your grounds is included in this chapter. Having explored what motivates children at play, we can work on more playful ways to engage them in learning, too.

It is interesting to consider that we are the only animals that teach formally! Cognitive scientists point out that intrinsic motivation for animals to learn involves curiosity, feeling competent and learning together. This is often demonstrated in playgrounds at playtimes, especially in natural play environments, with loose parts, non-specific structures and resources that afford multiple interpretations. So, why is this approach not more readily offered during curriculum time? There are several reasons that I have encountered, including teachers lacking confidence to work outside, senior leaders' skepticism and grounds that are not conducive to supporting outdoor learning.

Where there is wholehearted support for learning outside the classroom – where it is well embedded in planning and integrated into practice – then children are learning outdoors regularly and they thrive. This is what I observe in my work in schools. There is convincing evidence and plentiful anecdote that the quality and use of school grounds has a significant impact on children's learning and well-being, and thus on peaceful schools.

Recent research by Natural Connections[1] supports what many of us know from experience. The impact of Learning in the Natural Environment (LINE) on pupils was evaluated against the broad outcome areas identified by King's College London's evidence synthesis. The following percentage of respondents to the 2015 school survey agreed with the statement that LINE had a positive impact on pupils in the following aspects and percentages of respondents highlighting those aspects:

Enjoyment of lessons (95 per cent)

Connection to nature (94 per cent)

Social skills (93 per cent)

Engagement with learning (92 per cent)

Health and well-being (92 per cent)

Behaviour (85 per cent)

Attainment (57 per cent)

It is interesting to note that the apparently lower result on attainment was largely due to a lack of direct evidence rather than a lack of belief in the impact. In fact, those schools in the survey that had worked outdoors for many years reported measurable increases in attainment. One school gave an example where demonstrable improvements in children's written work had been underpinned by learning in the natural environment.

---

1   Waite, S., Passy, R., Gilchrist, M., Hunt, A. and Blackwell, I. (2016) *Natural Connections Demonstration Project, 2012–2016: Final Report*. Natural England Commissioned Reports, Number 215. 77. Manchester: Natural England.

There are many examples of studies, both anecdotal and academic research-based, that support what we see every day. For example, a study on children's mental and social health found that direct contact with nature, as facilitated by curriculum-based nature activities in schools, had a positive impact on self-esteem and mental health and well-being.

Health and well-being

Good quality play and recreation opportunities in school grounds deliver the benefits of better health and well-being outcomes for pupils/students and are also linked to a range of other developmental benefits. There is clear research evidence that constructive breaktime interventions deliver positive benefits in terms of children and young people's physical health, mental health, cognition and social skills. Access to the natural world in children's play and learning is so important and, as yet, many school grounds are still largely sterile environments that do not maximise their potential.

Canadian research was cited by Cam Collyer at the International School Grounds Alliance conference in Lund 2016. The headline was, 'The Biggest Risk to Children is Keeping Them Indoors', and this became the title of the ParticipACTION report card 2015, in which the following evidence is reported.

Ontario preschoolers spend twice as much time being active when play is outdoors (53 per cent of time active outdoors versus 23 per cent of time active indoors).

Students take 35 per cent more steps when a physical education class is held outdoors.

When children are outside, they move more, sit less and play longer and these are all behaviours associated with improved cholesterol levels, blood pressure, body composition, bone density, cardio-respiratory and musculoskeletal fitness and aspects of mental, social and environmental health. This research was led by health concerns, and schools can have a major role in giving children, whilst at school, a significant amount of time outdoors, whilst learning and playing.

So, how can we encourage high step-counts in playgrounds? The highest activity levels are recorded in what could be called 'flowing terrain', with changes in levels, mounds, slopes, steps and ramps, which all naturally require more cardiovascular effort to negotiate.

Children who do not enjoy sport will benefit particularly from play in this terrain, where they hardly know that they are exercising. A variety of places and spaces, with resources and 'play props' to manipulate, together with secure 'home bases' to start games from, afford many opportunities for all ages and abilities. Children respond well when given the freedom to invent games within non-specific environments that support active play.

The restorative power of the natural world is frequently discussed and observed. Although children have everyday access to tarmac and man-made materials, many city children and some rural children do not have gardens and some are not taken to parks and open spaces, so their only opportunity for contact with nature is in their school grounds. If you bring nature into the school grounds to give them a different experience, then more positive social play tends to occur as well.

Children with difficult or chaotic lives often benefit from time and a suitable place for reflection and exploration, where no demands are being made on them. This can help them to feel more peaceful. What is more, one-to-one interventions and support can be more effective in quiet 'safe spaces' outdoors. I am increasingly asked to design these into school grounds in order to supplement the interior nurture rooms.

Motivation and engagement with learning

So, how does the outdoors support motivation and child-centred learning? There are several key factors that children and staff tell me are important and that contribute to purposeful activity and peaceful school grounds:

- freedom of movement, due to more space to work in, especially for group work, and the team-building and bonding that ensues

- reduced constraints about noise, so fun and laughter are more welcome than indoors

- sensory engagement with the natural world and the seasons

- feeling calm is often cited by children because they feel less pressure to 'get it right' when they are working outside

- concepts can be experienced and learned before 'writing it down'

- a change of routine or pace is welcomed by many

- experience of the natural world and opportunities to observe at first hand

- relationships between children and adults are subtly different outdoors.

Active learning may help embed concepts for many children and the outdoor environment can be the best place for this – starting with an experience, and following it up in a classroom; for example, phonics collections outdoors with natural materials, or descriptive language developed during a 'micro-safari' in the grounds.

Children also learn effectively by seeing peers learn too, almost as a mirror to themselves, so pair work can build confidence, especially when learning about risk, taking care of oneself and others. An example of this is an anecdotal story about KS4 students working on a very practical project, where they used unfamiliar tools to construct garden benches. A reluctant girl watched her peers and then gained confidence to use a powered drill and screwdriver herself. It became apparent that she was very well able to do the task and took more care than some of the others. Her competence and confidence grew and she was very proud of her achievement.

Take another example – prepositions. These are important in Maths and are best learned physically...(before, after, above, below..., etc.) The interplay between the abstract and the concrete in outdoor activities using the whole body, in a number grid or number line, is more effective for some children than paper or cube-based indoor activities. The physical experience of moving to negative numbers along a line, for example, can reinforce a concept that can then be used in more formal class-based situations.

Design for positive behaviour and peaceful grounds

Schools are much more likely to be peaceful places if the outdoor environment is designed to promote positive behaviour and to meet the wide-ranging needs of everyone to have a rich learning environment with places of quiet, calm and reflection as well as places for boisterous, loud and busy activities.

Many teachers like to make use of the school grounds as a learning resource on a regular basis, but often find that the practicalities frustrate their ambitions. In Early Years settings, the culture and curriculum strongly support outdoor learning, and many schools aim to take elements of this forward into Key Stage 1, Key Stage 2 and beyond.

The teaching and learning function of school grounds should be a key design consideration. It is important to develop a strong brief for any changes through the participation of all 'stakeholders' (pupils, teachers and other school staff, parents and members of the local community) as well as drawing on expert advice and support. Involving teaching staff in generating a shared vision is one of the keys to success. It is worth noting that several headteachers have found that the engagement process itself can be very useful Continuing Professional Development (CPD) for their staff, challenging their thinking about what outdoor learning can look like across the whole curriculum and its influence on attainment and behaviour.

I would recommend looking at what other schools have done before you embark on your own school grounds improvement project. There are many good examples and inspirational models to learn from. The Organisations and Websites section at the end of this chapter can also help and inspire you to view your outdoor learning and play environment with fresh eyes.

As a teacher and landscape architect specialising in school grounds use and development, I have discovered that by applying the principles of spatial analysis, which are usually used for neighbourhood planning, to school grounds makes it possible to have a positive impact on the way the spaces work and how they feel to children and staff. Sadly, there are too many new-build and refurbished or extended schools where this approach was not undertaken in the planning stages. If it had been, then it could have influenced design decisions that, at no extra cost, could have had a positive effect on site dynamics, functionality, play and learning.

A site walkabout and observation of breaktimes always gives me a good understanding into the social and learning life of the pupils. I am particularly interested in the way in which children are influenced by the environment they are in. This is very relevant to the 'peaceful school' concept because the environment has a significant influence on children's behaviour and learning, which can be positive or negative.

Learning outside – a whole school ethos

It is important to remember that your whole school site is a learning resource, both inside and outside, offering different facilities to support different aspects of the curriculum and the development of children's knowledge and skills.

Do you worry that parents don't think that their children are learning when outside or that some children are reluctant to go outside? These concerns can be overcome, as the practice becomes part of the culture of the school and its way of working. A school community pulls together when the outcomes for children are clearly evident and evidenced. Skeptical parents/carers will see their children's attainment positively influenced by all that learning outdoors offers.

Your school prospectus, policies and open days when children explain how they work outdoors, all help to spread the understanding of why learning outside is important. If parents come into school for a workshop and learn outside with their children, they will experience it for themselves and see the benefits.

In one family literacy workshop that I led, the parents were surprised to be asked to work outside, collect natural materials, create a character and weave a story around that character. Their children joined them for 'storytime'. A fascinating mix of cultural references and imagination came out of this workshop, with parents going away enthused to talk with their children, invent stories with them and reduce 'screen time'! We know how important the parent is as first communicator and language builder for their children. This was just one way in which the outdoors helped to make this point strongly to the attendees.

Other examples of engaging parents include a nativity production in the woods, culminating with hot chocolate round the campfire, and another school had Santa's grotto in an open barn in the grounds instead of inside the school building during the Christmas fair.

Ofsted

Ofsted supports learning outside the classroom and states that it can improve the quality of teaching and engagement in learning across all areas of the curriculum: 'When planned and implemented well, learning outside the classroom contributed significantly to raising standards and improving pupils' personal, social and emotional development.'[2]

Ofsted produces good practice case studies on improving teaching and learning using the outdoor environment. Ofsted (2013) also suggests you should 'maintain curiosity' whilst delivering the science curriculum. How better to do this than working scientifically in the real world outside.[3]

Inclusive design and grounds maintenance for age, gender and ability

Did you know that excess colour can be 'dangerous'? So can confused patterns and bland amorphous spaces. Inclusive design too often thinks about physical disability above other cognitive and behavioural disorders. The character of a place is influenced by colour, texture and sound, and if any of these are 'strident', then the place can become disorientating, confusing and a source of anxiety rather than peace for some children.

Defined zones, clear routes, navigation and way-finding are important for all children but especially for visually impaired pupils/ students as well as for some of those on the autistic spectrum. My co-authored book with Laura Browning (2011), *Naturally Inclusive*, goes into this in further detail. Further design principles are discussed, including the importance of providing for all senses, including proprioceptive and vestibular.

A great tip when thinking about outdoor spaces for the youngest children, is to remember to get down to child's eye level and see a place from their point of view. This is especially important for Early Years and Key Stage 1. Appropriately chosen species of shrubs, with suitable pruning, can feel like a forest! One setting I worked on had a dense shrubbery that was never used. It was an obstacle to play. The children and I wielded saws and secateurs (with suitable risk–benefit assessment beforehand, of course) and opened up an 'explorer's route' through the shrubs. This has become a favorite retreat in a place that has a

---

2   'Learning outside the classroom: How far should you go?' OFSTED 2008 Ref 070219 p.5. Accessed 28 November 2017 at www.lotc.org.uk/wp-content/ uploads/2010/12/Ofsted-Report-Oct-2008.pdf.

3   Maintaining Curiosity: A Survey into Science Education in Schools. (Manchester: Ofsted, 2013).

very different character to the main play area. Vocabulary development through experience of this new natural resource is evident.

Grounds maintenance and management can make or break the vision of school grounds. A shared understanding of the importance and potential of school grounds is essential to its success in a peaceful school. Try to employ sensitive maintenance staff, who can prune restoratively, think in child scale and understand the site as a learning resource. You may want to review the job description of the site manager, and elements of the grounds maintenance specification, too, in order to be sure that everyone understands the character and purpose of every space in the grounds. I have all too often heard of embryonic wild-flower meadows being strimmed by contractors just as they were about to come into flower! Our valuable pollinating insects were not impressed and the grounds were certainly not peaceful when the children found out!

Play and recreation

Tim Gill, a respected commentator on play, observes that if the four key factors of appropriate space, time, other children and a supportive adult attitude are in place, then it is reasonable to expect that health and developmental benefits will result.[4] Taken as a whole, research findings make a strong case for a more sustained focus on what is arguably a neglected and undervalued time in children's lives. The audit suggested below gives you a useful structure to focus your review of your playgrounds.

It is also very interesting to see children, during their play, re-enacting a story, or a learning task that they first did outdoors during lesson times. Play versions reinforce the learning very effectively, giving children an opportunity to teach one another in an informal way. This will only happen outdoors at play if the original version took place outdoors in the same environment.

'Loose Parts' play is, I believe, a very useful tool for fostering peaceful productive activity in school grounds for learning as well as for play. In my experience, the introduction of a wide range of natural and modular resources such as logs, planks, cargo nets, crates,

---

4   Gill, T. (2014) *The Play Return: A Review of the Wider Impact of Play Initiatives.* New Barnet: The Children's Play Policy Forum.

well-chosen scrap and props, inject a new positive atmosphere into the grounds. Sufficient quantity and variety, careful introduction, training and modelling of the use of these resources are the key to success. At one primary school, I observed a Year 5 teacher working with her class using the abundant loose parts that I had recently introduced. Each team of five children had to design and build an obstacle course, then draw it, roughly to scale, and then add a key to their plan. What a great introduction to the rudiments of maps and plans. This was play and learning combined very effectively. No disruptive behaviour was observed…peace reigned and children learned!

Your own school grounds
Site audit – understanding your outdoor space

The whole site, buildings and landscape, are learning resources that should be thought of as a whole so as to ensure that the resources are used effectively. When staff see that indoors and outdoors complement each other, the children's perspectives are challenged, too, and they begin to see outdoors as a learning place as well as a play space. This does not need to mean extra expenditure on the grounds. Most schools already have a wide range of resources, plants, leaves, twigs, trees, places, spaces, surfaces and materials that support learning. Here is a checklist of questions to help you audit your own school grounds.

The starting point for making improvements/changes should be to ask the questions below, involving the whole school community:

- What currently works well in the grounds, and what are the missing experiences?

- Are there enough places of different character to support learning and play, including access to the natural world? Key to success is 'place-making' (i.e. defining versatile spaces of different character) in order to meet the many and varying needs of pupils, as well as the needs that staff have for teaching, as well as sports and play. Remember that 'play' is still important at secondary level, too.

- Where are the calm, peaceful places and the open boisterous places? Do these need further definition to enhance their character and purpose?

- Think about pedestrian traffic flow. Are there any points of congestion?

- Where are the 'trouble spots' and how can these be reimagined as positive spaces and places?

- Whose needs are marginalised or not being met at playtime? Observers need to consider the social, emotional and physical needs of pupils as well as the curriculum requirements for sports and other subjects.

- Are your midday staff play leaders or play supervisors? Do you need to review their job descriptions? The most effective midday staff facilitate and support play, rather than just supervise it. Well-trained and respected by the children, they are a huge asset. Their job descriptions should reflect this expectation. Surveillance and supervision are two very different concepts. The attitude of supporting adults can have a significant impact on site dynamics and behaviour.

- What is the school ethos and policy around play and outdoor learning? Is this well understood by all staff and the parent community?

- When you have identified the key issues, think about how students can be involved in developing and implementing solutions.

Observation

The pupils at any school are the site experts. It is in observing them and talking to them that you can get 'under the skin' of the site and its characteristics. An outside eye is often helpful to see the big picture as you may be too close to really see the issues and potential of your own site. Heads and governors often tell me that the outside overview that I bring is highly valued and helps them to see their grounds with new eyes.

There are many aspects of the school grounds that should be audited in order to get a full picture of how well the grounds are meeting needs. For example, much can be learned from how a site is 'colonised' when the pupils come out for break; what the key routes are around the site; nodes and congestion points; places where people congregate and what they do in these congregations. You can also spot the students or activities that are marginalised by other activities (often ball games) or by site design that has not taken their needs into account.

Areas of damage, accidental or otherwise, very often tell a site design story, too. Another key indicator is to look at how much of the site gives the students an opportunity to manipulate their environment in a positive way to suit their needs. The versatility of spaces for learning, as well as social times, is very important to the functionality and peacefulness of the grounds.

Continuum of activity

When rethinking your outdoor space, the 'continuum of activity' design principle can be useful as it helps to improve the quality of activity all around play spaces by ensuring that neighbouring activities do not impinge negatively on each other, thus reducing conflicts. At one end of the continuum are the quieter, more focused activities and at the other end are faster, more physical activities.

During your audit, identify your existing zones on a site plan and apply this continuum. Are there key points where conflicts occur? This is a useful guiding principle to think about when planning changes to any school grounds.

Well-defined and resourced spaces will enhance the focus of the activity within that space. For example, a mud kitchen is a great resource for Early Years and primary children, and has a clear purpose, at the quieter end of the spectrum. However, if it is defined by structures with an ambiguous purpose conflict can occur. I have seen tyres and planks at different levels used as a boundary around a mud kitchen, but these were too inviting for children to use for more active 'parcour' play; these interfered with the quality of activity around the mud kitchen and an adjacent small world/loose parts play area. These tyres and planks would be best taken out of this 'quieter' end of the continuum into an area better suited to more active play. Opportunities for graduated challenges and obstacle courses could then be designed by the children with a large resource bank of suitable modular resources. This provides a degree of risk and challenge that can be planned to be suitable to all ages. Locating this away from the mud kitchen, at the other end of the continuum, enhances the play in both areas.

Zones

Think about zones and the expectations of activities and behaviour in different parts of the school's learning environment, inside and outside. Zones do not have to be rigid and lacking in versatility, with the exception of ball courts perhaps. The best places are simply areas with good boundaries, within which a range of imaginative activities can take place. These can be defined with appropriate and versatile structures, including zone-specific storage units that encourage independent use of equipment by the children. This will take time to establish of course, but with consistency of message it can and will happen!

Aim for the provision of a wide variety of versatile places with different characters such as more intimate natural dens (with good surveillance) with a range of surface textures, planting, sensory input, visual texture and materials that will also be useful learning resources.

It may help to reinforce the character of each place and the activity within it if there is more consideration given to appropriate play props and resourcing. Definition of space and naming the 'zones' appropriately/more imaginatively can help, too. For example, new names are needed in situations when primary schools combine previously distinct Key Stage 1 and Key Stage 2 playgrounds, but still persist in calling them 'infants' and 'juniors', even when the areas are no longer solely used by those age ranges.

Renaming can have positive impacts on activity and a shared understanding of expectations. Some areas are readily named by the children according to the activity taking place, such as Mud Kitchen, Stage, Ball Courts, Amphitheatre, Den Village, etc. Children will no doubt come up with good names for your key zones; if the names are consistently used by everyone, they will in time reinforce the expectations of activity/behaviour in each zone.

Engaging children in the identification of issues, developing solutions and making changes helps to embed the zones in the everyday life of the school. The children take great pride in doing this work.

Engagement

Consultation is different from engagement. I feel that consultation is largely passive, whereas engagement is more active and offers a purposeful application of skills. Wherever possible, I recommend that the whole school community is engaged in the process of auditing, identifying issues, generating ideas and finding solutions. Surprisingly, this is not about asking what children 'want' in the playground, or to 'design their ideal playground'. Neither task really gets to the bottom of what needs changing! What is important is to ask children and staff what they want to be able to DO in the grounds. This is a subtly different question.

An essential component of any school grounds assessment is to have conversations within the school community about everyone's current experiences of the grounds and their aspirations for the future of the school. Staff and governors have said to me that debating the vision for outdoors has helped them to clarify what they really required from their grounds and reduced wasted expenditure on things that did not meet need.

This is an opportunity to engage pupils in 'real-world' learning. They can be involved as researchers, surveyors, problem-solvers and designers. They can get engaged in construction too, from laying paving to wood carving and planting. Children of any age can get involved in these activities. As an example, I asked a nursery class to help the contractors to move a huge (to them) bag of topsoil from its delivery location to the planting bed. They pondered the problem and suggested a variety of solutions. Then they deployed a wide range of transporting resources such as buckets, wheeled toys and, to greatest effect, a trailer towed by a trike. The driver of the trike took his job very seriously and persisted in this task for most of the morning. He waited while his friend loaded his trailer, then he cycled it to the planting bed and waited while it was unloaded before taking the empty trailer back for reloading. That day in the nursery playground, the atmosphere was peaceful and purposeful! The children took great pride in 'being builders' for real, not just role playing.

Site redesign

Site redesign projects, and the engagement of students during the process, need to be carefully tailored to each school, the age of the pupils and specific curriculum needs or outcomes related to work and careers (for the older students). Expert assistance will be invaluable to make the project happen. You may be wondering if large budgets are required – not necessarily, and whatever budget you have is better spent in the context of a well-considered overall master plan rather than piecemeal. Remember, too, that any funders will want to see evidence of need and pupil engagement to persuade them to help to fund your project.

Workshops for staff and pupils facilitated by specialist consultants can help in the development of the project. Any school grounds development project, large or small, is a great opportunity for children and young people to make a positive contribution to their school and feel pride in a tangible achievement.

Conclusion

In conclusion, I just want to restate that the grounds of a peaceful school will be well used and managed, with a successful combination of a shared vision, positive relationships and positive environments for teaching, learning, play, recreation and life-skills development!

References

Dillon, J. and Dickie, I. (2012) *Learning in the Natural Environment: Review of Social and Economic Benefits and Barriers.* Natural England Commissioned Reports, Number 092. Manchester: Natural England.

International Journal of Environmental Research and Public Health ISSN (2016) 1660-4601 para 3.1 p 6483. Accessed 29 November 2017 at www.mdpi.com/journal/ijerph.

Kuo, F.E. and Sullivan, W.C. (2001) 'Aggression and violence in the inner city: Effects of environment via mental fatigue.' *Environment and Behaviour* 33: 543–571.

Ofsted (2013) *Maintaining Curiosity: A Survey into Science Education in Schools.* Manchester: Ofsted.

ParticipACTION (2015) *The Biggest Risk is Keeping Kids Indoors.* The 2015 ParticipACTION Report Card on Physical Activity for Children and Youth. Toronto: ParticipACTION. Accessed 29 November 2017 at www.participactionreportcard.com.

Robinson, F. and Browning, L. (2011) *Naturally Inclusive: An Approach to Design for Play.* Winchester: Learning through Landscapes.

Vanderloo, L.M., Tucker, P., Johnson, A.M. and Holmes, J.D. (2013) 'Physical activity among preschoolers during indoor and outdoor childcare play periods.' *Applied Physiology, Nutrition and Metabolism* 38: 1173–1175.

Organisations and websites

The 'Council for Learning Outside the Classroom' is the national voice for learning outside the classroom. www.lotc.org.uk

'Landscapes Naturally' (Felicity Robinson) supports schools to transform outdoor learning and play and promotes education through engagement in grounds development projects at small and large scale. She can also help you with grant applications and fundraising. Felicity works nationally and internationally. www.landscapesnaturally.co.uk

'Learning through Landscapes' helps children to connect with nature, become more active, learn outdoors, develop social skills and have fun. www.ltl.org.uk

CHAPTER 8

PEACEFUL PLAYTIMES

Thérèse Hoyle

Introduction

Over the last 20 years, I have been running and developing Positive Playtime and Lunchtime Training Programmes to support schools with making this a peaceful and harmonious time in the school day. I remember in the early days, I developed a three-day masterclass that I first ran in a South London school. To this day, I have visions of myself as a heavily pregnant first-time mum, sitting cross-legged on the concrete playground playing 'Duck, duck, goose'! My daughter is now 19! Since then, I have written two books: *101 Playtime Games* (2008) and *101 Wet Playtime Games and Activities* (2009), and have worked nationally and internationally with over 450 schools and organisations and with more than 14,500 individuals and countless numbers of children! I have learned so much on my journey and I am excited to share this with you.

I have a huge passion to meet the social and emotional needs of our children and tackle the areas of weakness in schools that stop children learning partly because of my own childhood experiences and also because, in the work I do, children share their heartfelt stories and challenges, and these frequently centre on unhappy playtimes and lunchtimes. For me, the happy playtimes at primary school were when I was included, played games and had fun. I can still remember skipping with elastics (French skipping), the game 'The big ship sails on the alley alley oh!' and gymnastics on the field. Those were the good times and then there were the days where I felt like an outsider, feeling that I had no friends and that no one wanted to play with me. I would wander round the playground feeling like a spare part, lonely and sad. Secondary school was different – we had wide-open spaces and I loved the freedom of our playground, the woods where we played and the friendships I formed.

Peaceful playtime experiences are essential to the development of students' social skills and in creating a safe, learning culture throughout the school. Through play, children develop and build relationships and social skills, de-stress and let off steam, exercise and most of all have fun. The aim of this chapter is to give you some theoretical underpinnings as to the value and importance of play and then, as I do on my training days, provide you with simple steps to implement a peaceful playtime programme in your school. The chapter covers Early Years, primary, secondary and special needs schools.

How much time do children spend playing?

Have you ever stopped to think about how much time children spend in the playground? It is approximately 20 per cent of their school day. Over the course of their primary schooling, from Reception to Year 6, children spend over 1,600 hours playing, which equates to 260 school days. That is pretty significant and it may make you rethink the investment that you put into your outdoor learning environment. Your school will benefit from working out how to make this a positive and peaceful time in the school day because what happens in the playground affects the whole life of the school, including the children's ability to learn.

What is a peaceful playtime?

A peaceful playtime is about creating an environment that is peaceful and playful where children can flourish, play happily and harmoniously – safe and free from conflict and bullying. So, wouldn't it be wonderful if every school playtime was like this? I visit schools where this becomes the reality because they choose to invest time, resources and energy into making it happen.

Playtime problems

Many headteachers, teachers and lunchtime supervisors on my Positive Playtime courses tell me, their playtimes are far from peaceful, with children struggling with friendship issues, bullying and boredom because of a lack of resources, and some children just do not know how to play. The honest truth is that many schools struggle with this time in the school day.

I spend time in schools all over the country running playtime and lunchtime programmes, talking with hundreds of children in Circle Time about what is going well with playtimes as well as their worries and concerns. Their worries fall into the following categories:

- Friendship – lack of friends, being left out of games, asking to play a game and being told 'no' they can't join in, friends being unkind and arguing

- Lack of things to do – boredom stemming from not enough equipment or things to do in the playground

- Feeling unsafe – physical and verbal aggression.

Research shows us that 75 per cent of bullying happens in the school playground (Smith and Sharp 1994), and one of the suggested causes is boredom or lack of stimulus. More recent research has found that children are four times more likely to be bullied in the school playground than online. The effects of bullying, as we know, can have a painful and lifelong impact, and we need to do all that we can in our schools in order to create peaceful playtimes and safeguard our children.

The benefits to children of creating a positive and peaceful playtime

For learning

Creating a safe, peaceful, nurturing school is vital to our children achieving their potential and to meeting Ofsted requirements around safeguarding, pupil behaviour, discipline, child welfare and quality teaching and learning. Teachers and parents want children to be safe and to learn, but children can develop emotional barriers to learning as a result of bad playtime and lunchtime experiences. Upsets can be taken back into the classroom after lunch and it can be hard to engage children in schoolwork with all their thoughts still focused on the challenges they have experienced.

Social, emotional and mental well-being

It is increasingly understood that play makes a significant contribution to children's well-being in terms of their mental, social, emotional and spiritual well-being. Peaceful playtimes can be the time in the day when many children can let go of worries and concerns and engage in fun activities. Positive, physical, interactive play is very important to long-term emotional health.

Psychologists and researchers have found what makes people happy: to have good relationships with other human beings, to do work you like and to be a contributing member of a community. When children play, they develop and build good relationships, do work they love and contribute to the school community. The positive emotions that come from positive play and positive social interaction lead to the production of good chemicals in children's bodies – such as opioids and oxytocin, which make them feel calm, content, secure and safe; dopamine, which is the 'motivation chemical', and serotonin, the well-being, 'feel-good' chemical that is a major factor in social and emotional intelligence.

In her article 'The Serious Need for Play', science health journalist Melinda Wenner (2009) concludes that: 'Free, imaginative play is crucial for normal social, emotional and cognitive development. It makes us better adjusted, smarter and less stressed.' She highlights that 'kids and animals that do not play when they are young may grow into anxious, socially maladjusted adults'. She mentions the work of psychiatrist Stuart Brown, who has interviewed some 6,000 people about their childhoods and his data suggests that a lack of opportunities for unstructured, imaginative play can keep children from growing into happy, well-adjusted adults. 'Free play,' as scientists call it, is critical for becoming socially adept, coping with stress and building cognitive skills such as problem-solving. The Department of Health's report, *At Least Five a Week: Evidence on the Impact of Physical Activity and its Relationship to Health* (2004), substantiates these findings, saying that children benefit from physically active play in terms of their mental health, and that children with lower physical activity levels have more symptoms of psychological distress than more active children.

Physical health and well-being

When children and young people exercise in the form of running around in the playground and playing games, it improves their emotional health and sense of peacefulness, allowing for relaxation and calmness and a heightened sense of well-being. It is also, as we know, vital for children, in terms of their physical health and well-being. Physical activity has dramatic effects on individuals' physical and mental health (Basch 2011). Playing reduces their chances of being obese. The World Health Organization regards childhood obesity as one of the most serious global public health challenges of the twenty-first century. Obese children are more likely to develop childhood diabetes, along with various other health problems. This, along with the news that doctors have started prescribing vitamin D tablets to children following an upsurge in the number of children developing rickets through lack of sunshine, is astonishing, when playing outside offers a simple and easy way to significantly reduce the chances of experiencing these health problems.

Sadly, some schools are shortening playtimes, when a longer playtime would allow children to gain the most benefit from physical activity, as studies have found that higher physical activity levels were associated with longer playtimes. We want our children to be walking, running, laughing and happy during their playtime, every school day. Their health will be significantly stronger as a result.

Creating a peaceful playtime

Conduct an audit to assess your school's 'state of play'

When we are creating a more peaceful playtime, it is important to spend time observing children at play, to look at all available space and initially assess how peaceful the current play provision and space is. Many schools complete audits that are useful and help them measure their effectiveness. The audit can help to identify strengths, weaknesses, opportunities and areas for future development, and threats such as health and safety issues, holes in fences, unsafe playground equipment, etc. Ideally, the whole school should be consulted – children, staff and parents. Once you have completed this exercise, celebrate your school's strengths and look at the areas of weakness, threats and possible opportunities. From that, you can formulate an action plan that can be part of the School's Development Plan.

Create Playtime Activity Zones

I have seen many a featureless, concrete playground environment transformed into a peaceful, thriving, creative, active and engaging play space 'Playtime Activity Zone', with just a bit of thought and imagination. Ideas for zoned activity areas include:

- imaginative play zone

- traditional playground games zone

- 'friendship stop' zone

- quiet zone

- activity of the week (one type of equipment is used every day of the week)

- construction/small world play equipment

- ball games – football, netball, basketball

- parachute games

- performing arts – a music and dance zone

- painted on the ground or walls games – hopscotch, etc.

Activity of the Week

The 'Activity of the Week' is a very successful lunchtime strategy. A new and exciting activity is played for a week and then put away. A fresh new activity is put out the following week.

In order to organise the activity of the week:

- First of all, talk with the children about activities that they would love to have in the playground.

- Choose and buy enough equipment for that activity. Activities can be things such as skipping ropes, French skipping ropes, bean bags, plastic stilts, whoppas, ankle skips, shuttleball, hoops, lolo ball, cat's cradle, etc. There is so much equipment for children to choose from and I would suggest going through a catalogue with them and deciding on the most popular activities. You will need roughly 10–15 of each, depending on the size of your school, and these will then create your playground activity boxes.

- Create an 'Activity of the Week' noticeboard that is alternated each week, for example: 'Our activity this week is skipping.'

- Every week, on Monday morning, introduce the activity of the week in assembly.

Peaceful zone

Do any of these scenarios sound familiar? Are there children in your school who:

- don't enjoy running around at playtimes?

- would rather sit in quiet contemplation, maybe in a quiet area of the playground or a garden or more solitary space?

- would prefer to read a book or play a peaceful game or activity?

If you have answered 'yes' to any of the above, then it is time to create a 'peaceful zone' space and offer the choice of quieter games and activities. Educationally, it is important that we offer children a breadth of experience and playtime is no exception. Here are some ideas:

- Teach all children the quiet games from *101 Playground Games* (Hoyle 2008) in their PE lessons.

- Create a peaceful zoned activity area, with picnic tables, rugs and mats when the weather permits.

- Organise 'Quiet Games Activity' boxes for the peaceful zoned area. These may include: cat's cradle, wooden dominoes, Jenga, giant noughts and crosses, pick-up sticks, tiddlywinks, board games, Lego, cards, colouring-in and bricks.

- Create a secret garden or quiet space away from the busy playground. If you have access to a green area or garden, then this is perfect.

- Develop a gardening club for the children who like to connect with nature at playtime.

Early Years and Key Stage 1

In my experience, there is often a huge jump for Key Stage 1 (KS1) children, from the secure nursery and reception playgrounds to the huge and often daunting large primary school play space. Reflect for a moment on how good the transition is in your school from Early Years to KS1, in terms of playtime resources for your young children. In creating a smooth transition, I would suggest creating an imaginative play area, where they use playground equipment such as:

- road-track sets

- giant plastic playing cards

- colouring-in books

- dressing-up boxes

- tower and Cube set (like polydron, however huge!)

- Lego and big build blocks

- Small World Play.

This will lead to an easier transition, more peaceful playtimes and happy, contented children at play.

Transition to secondary school

Many of the ideas suggested for primary students are also applicable to secondary students. For secondary students, transitioning to secondary school can be a worrying time and playtimes can cause anxiety with feelings of: 'Will I have anyone to play with today?' or 'Will I get left out of games?' or 'I don't want to join a club' and so on. Students in Year 7 often tell me that when they get to secondary school, there is not enough to do at playtimes and all sorts of problems occur, which means that playtime is far from peaceful. I suggest that secondary schools ask their students what activities they would like to have. Many students do not enjoy getting involved in the lunchtime sports and would rather play games such as skipping, ball games, tag games, etc. Some really enjoy a peaceful zone, like in primary school, where they can read or play a board game. A peaceful garden or chill zone can also prove very popular at secondary school.

As we can see, not only do children enjoy playing and playtimes, but they also learn a great deal through games and activities. Playtimes and lunchtimes, then, are not simply an excuse for children to run around and let off steam. In many ways, they are also part of the educational and social development of the child – an extension of the classroom. Children from ethnic backgrounds and children with disabilities benefit from 'play' at playtime, in terms of social development and inclusion. Blatchford and others (2003) found that playtimes have the potential to enable children from different ethnic groups to play together. It is interesting to note that it has been suggested that afternoon playtimes and playtimes that allow mixed-age groups to play together could improve the inclusion of children with disabilities in the playground.

Developing behaviour management systems that foster peaceful playtimes

Without clear rules and boundaries, I do not believe that we can have peace! Getting your behaviour management systems sorted is essential to providing children with a secure, bully-free environment that fosters happy, calm and peaceful playtimes. I strongly believe that one of the reasons that playtimes can be a challenging and non-peaceful time in the school day is because we spend most of our time focusing on teaching and learning and our internal school systems, and we forget about learning outside the classroom and our lunchtimes and playtimes. Most headteachers I work with know that if we do not get this time in the school day right, then children suffer in the afternoon and are unable to learn. The behaviour of the children inside the school maybe outstanding, but the opposite may be the case in the playground. Research tells us that more and more schools are worried about deteriorating behaviour at playtime (Blatchford and Baines 2006; Pellegrini and Blatchford 2002).

I encourage schools to review their playtime and lunchtime behaviour management systems. Lunchtime supervisors frequently tell me that the systems inside the school are excellent, yet those outside are poor, unclear or non-existent, and this then leads them to feeling ineffective and powerless. Outlined here are some simple steps that I use with schools on my training days. I hope that they will support you in making playtimes and lunchtimes a safe and peaceful time for everyone.

Rules

One of the most important things to sort out at playtime is your school and playtime rules. Schools are fantastic at having clear codes of conduct, values and rules displayed inside our school buildings and classrooms, but can often forget to do this when it comes to our outside spaces. If this is the case, then children start to think that there is a different set of moral values inside to outside! So, if you do not have rules for the outdoor areas, then you could look at your current rules and adapt them for the playground. I like rules that cover the 4Rs of:

- respect for self
- respect for others
- respect for property and the environment
- responsibility for all your actions.

At the start of the academic year, schools generally have an assembly welcoming everyone back and reinforcing the school rules, which might have been forgotten over the six-week summer break. It is important for every member of staff to be invited to this assembly, so that the children see that the whole school staff know what the rules are and that everyone is working together. Children will often think that MSAs (Midday Supervisory Assistants) do not know the school rules and so will try and lead them a little dance. The reward of good playground behaviour is that they 'always get to have fun!' However, in order to incentivise children, there are many rewards on the market, from lunchtime stickers to reward slips and certificates.

It is important that a peaceful problem-solving, solution-focused culture is developed in a school. This can be done through things like weekly Circle Time and schemes like peer mediation and playtime pals. Lunchtime supervisors are encouraged to help pupils sort out problems in a peaceful, fair way and encourage pupils to take responsibility for their behaviour. They should listen to all parties involved and encourage pupils to problem-solve and find solutions. In some circumstances, staff will intervene and help both parties reach a fair and amicable agreement.

In my Positive Playtimes Masterclass, I run Circle Time sessions with the children and the school staff observe. The aim of these sessions is for me to find out what is going well at playtimes and the behaviours children are struggling with. Circle Time helps develop peaceful problem-solving skills, communication and social skills. I suggest to schools that there is an ongoing timetable of Circle Time and that it is held once a week at a set time.

Consequences vary from school to school. Most schools agree that there needs to be some sort of restorative consequence, such as time for the student to think through how they could have acted and how they could choose to behave differently next time, as well as time to restore relationships that may have broken down. In the first instance, with low-level incidences, a verbal warning is often all that is needed. However, if the child breaks the rule again, 5–10 minutes of 'time out to think' is a good consequence. The child usually has to sit in a solitary place, on a bench, in the hall or classroom, away from other children, thinking through which rule they have broken and which rule they need to be keeping and who they may need to apologise to. Children can join in the game or activity once they have had time out and/or as long as relationships have been restored.

You may know some children who are hugely reactive at playtime. Danger, stress and anxiety trigger the release of adrenalin and cortisol, which often leads to the fight-or-flight response.

These children do not have the stress-regulating brain chemicals to calm themselves and need soothing, calming adults to help regulate the chemicals that have flooded their brains.

Positive play experiences and positive social interaction for these children lead to positive emotions, which can make them feel more peaceful.

Lunchtime supervisors

Lunchtime supervisors are essential to the smooth running of any lunchtime and we need to ensure that that they are well-trained and supported. I frequently teach lunchtime supervisors the PLACE model developed by American child psychologist Dr Dan Hughes, which supports them with building positive relationships with the children. Hughes believes that your attitude to the child is key and that your relationship with the child is crucial to them developing a positive sense of self and self-esteem. Remember to be:

P = Playful

L = Loving

A = Accepting

C = Curious

E = Empathic

Playground Activity Leaders (PALS) for peaceful playtimes

PALS consist of a group of children who help make the playground a safer, more peaceful place for younger children. Their responsibilities are to:

- teach children different games

- befriend lonely children and help them make friends

- take out and put away playground equipment.

All members of the playground PALS team meet regularly with the teacher responsible for playtimes for training and ongoing support. The PALS wear special tabards or caps for ease of identification.

When considering adopting this system in your school, please give consideration to:

- how many PALS you will need, given the size of your playground and number of children in your school

- how many times a week it would be suitable for them to be out on games duty

- how would the PALS be chosen

- what support they will need.

Training pupils to become PALS should ideally be done by a teaching assistant, lunchtime supervisor or a teacher who will take responsibility for the PALS, their training and on going support. I would suggest teaching PALS a selection of games. If you have a copy of *101 Playground Games* (Hoyle 2008), print out the 'Traditional Playground Games' section from the CD ROM or download the free version from www.theresehoyle.com and give each child a pack of games that they can keep and use as a reference. This will give the PALS ten playground games to learn and introduce to other children. At the end of term or their time as a PAL, they receive a certificate to thank them for their contribution and hard work. This is given out in assembly.

Finally

The best way to create a peaceful playtime is to have a whole school programme, with everyone working together towards the same goals and aims, creating a great school where everyone feels safe, peaceful and able to learn.

References

Basch C. (2011) 'Healthier students make better learners.' *Journal of School Health*, Wiley Online Library. Accessed 15 December 2017 available at https://scholar.google.co.uk/scholar?q=Basch+C.+(2011)+'Healthier+students+make+better+learners.'+Journal+of+School+Health,+Wiley+Online+Library.%5B&hl=en&as_sdt=0&as_vis=1&oi=scholart&sa=X&ved=0ahUKEwj_qaC17vLXAhVKI8AKHXRcDxIQgQMIJzAA.

Blatchford, P. and Baines, E. (2006) *A Follow Up National Survey of Breaktimes in Primary and Secondary Schools.* London: Institute of Education.

Blatchford, P., Baines, E. and Pellegrini, A. (2003) 'The social context of school playground games: Sex and ethnic differences, and changes over time after entry to junior school.' *British Journal of Developmental Psychology 21*, 481–505.

Department of Health (2004) *At Least Five a Week: Evidence on the Impact of Physical Activity and its Relationship to Health.*

Hoyle, T. (2008) *101 Playground Games.* London: Optimus Education.

Hoyle, T. (2009) *101 Wet Playtime Games and Activities.* London: Optimus Education.

Pellegrini, A. and Blatchford, P. (2002) 'Time for a break.' *The Psychologist 15*, 2, 60–62.

Smith, P.K. and Sharp, S. (eds) (1994) *School Bullying: Insights and Perspectives.* London: Routledge.

Wenner, M. (2009) 'The serious need for play.' *The Scientific American Mind*, 28 January 2009.

Further Reading

Blatchford, P., Pellegrini, A., Baines, E. and Kentaro, K. (2002) *Playground Games: Their Social Context in Elementary/Junior school.* Final Report to the Spencer Foundation Chicago, IL.

CHAPTER 9

OUR PEACEFUL SCHOOL COMMUNITY

Wendy Phillips

Introduction

St Andrew's Catholic Primary School is located at the heart of Streatham in South West London and it is one of the first Beacon Peaceful Schools in the UK. Our school welcomes over 500 children from our local parishes. Their families represent many different countries from around the world. We are proud to embrace the many cultures and traditions, and over 30 languages that make up the diverse and vibrant community of our school. As with many changing communities across the country, we have had to take special care to ensure that everyone feels valued, respected and loved for who they are. We seek to enable everyone – children, staff and families – to help to create a community where we stand together and open our hearts to everyone.

St Andrew's is a Catholic school and we are very conscious that, for us, religion is not just a subject, but it is also a way of life. Our Gospel values of Praying, Sharing, Forgiving and Telling the Truth are a lived reality. Every aspect of the school reflects this, so that, by its very nature, the school contributes to the life of the parish and the community.

I had the pleasure of being appointed as a Learning Mentor in this amazing school over 16 years ago, with my role being to break down any barriers to learning. I have been fortunate enough to work under the guidance of the school's inspiring Headteacher, Denise Assid, with her mission to make this school a place where children are offered the very best education that they can have and know that all the staff love them and want them to be the very best that they can be in their learning, relationships and their communities. This motivated me to work alongside her in order to make this happen.

My passion for peace is to empower our children to understand that life has no calendar and sad things can happen in their lives when we do not expect them to. We have worked to find practical ways to enable them to manage these experiences and find the inner peace and strength to manage them.

In this chapter, you will read about how we have worked with our school community and other charities to put peace at the centre of everything that we do. You will read about examples of how we have embedded the message of peace in practical and inclusive ways.

From inner peace to a peaceful community

In order to achieve a peaceful community, we strongly believe that we need to nurture a culture where children, staff and parents can recognise what inner peace means to each of them and how we, as a school community, can collectively embody this vision of inner peace so that it becomes 'just what we do around here'.

Every child in our school truly matters and we seek out every opportunity to enable pupils to know that they are unique, special, loved by God and respected within our school community for who they are. We start with 'self' and work with our children in order to explore questions such as: What things are important to you? What things can help you to feel safe? How can this be shared with others?

We encourage children to acknowledge all their feelings and understand that there are no 'wrong' feelings or emotions. We explain that it is important that we all understand that, no matter how we are feeling, we must find a respectful manner to express our feelings, so that our actions do not put ourselves or others at risk, for example by losing control of our behaviour. We have a motto: 'You have a right to feel safe and others have a right to feel safe with you.' This is reinforced and discussed through circle times, PSHE lessons, special focus weeks, assemblies and RE lessons.

At times, some of our families have gone through changes due to bereavement, family breakdown or long-term illness. These changes can cause some families to withdraw from the community as they do not know how to cope or put their feelings into words to their children. We have an after-school club called 'Rainbows', which has been established for over ten years. It is a safe space that allows children to explore their feelings, share their news – good or bad – and express their feelings and thoughts through role play, discussions, art and prayers. At the end of each term, the children invite a member of their family to our final session. This gives both the children and their guests the opportunity to express how they have benefitted from attending the club. As the facilitator, it allows me the opportunity to reinforce the message that, although their families have changed, they are still special and important and their feelings count.

Further to this club, the children decided that they would like to have a space where they could reflect, pray and remember the people in their lives who have died. We decided to create a 'Peace Garden'. It has a special noticeboard that they can use to display their prayers, pictures and religious artefacts. There is a special wall that has plaques to commemorate parents and members of our school community who have died. The Peace Garden has a pond with fish that the children like very much. They say that it makes them feel calm and relaxed being near the water. There are stained-glass religious artworks that the pupils designed and we had made up, so that on sunny days, these images shine into our garden.

The Peace Garden is also open to parents. It is a nice quiet space that they can use to speak to their children if they have to tell them sad news. Teachers also use it as a place that children can go to if they need some thinking time away from others, where they can be surrounded by comforting images and words.

One of the most powerful tools that we use across the school is our 'Talk Boxes'. These boxes are used as a way for children to share their positive news as well as things that may be concerning them. The entries in the box are anonymous and the children are encouraged to offer advice to each other about how to manage these situations. These boxes also form part of our Lenten class reflections, when the pupils are able to reflect on what has been challenging for them and what steps they are going to take during Lent in order to be calm, compassionate, caring and following in the footsteps of Jesus.

We have children who have been trained up as 'Playground Buddies'. Their jobs are to ensure that playtimes are fun and inclusive for all. They are trained to use restorative approaches to conflict resolution and to be visible peer helpers in the playground.

Many years ago, the staff came up with a mission statement that was worded using rather adult language. We undertook a process of consultation to come up with a child-friendly version. We talked to the School Council and asked classes to come up with their own wording. This meant that the children were able to take ownership of the mission statement and they can now refer to it in a way that is meaningful to them. Once we had this in place, it was unveiled as a beautiful focal point in our reception area and is displayed in every class.

St Andrew's Mission Statement

St Andrew's School is a place where:

> We feel safe.
>
> We know that we are special.
>
> We know God loves us.
>
> God's love is alive here.
>
> We pray together.
>
> We share with each other.
>
> We forgive one another.
>
> We tell the truth.
>
> We enjoy our learning.
>
> We are rewarded for our efforts in both work and behaviour.
>
> We show respect for each person's ability, country and language.
>
> We aim high.
>
> Our achievements are excellent.
>
> We are valued.
>
> We are respected.
>
> Together, we help make our school, our neighbourhood and the world a better place.

Putting our mission statement into practice

We talked with the children about how we could transfer the messages from the mission statement into the everyday life of the school. The pupils' School Council came up with the idea of having a 'Focus of the Week' that would link to our 'Peace Maker' certificates, which are awarded every week at our Reward Assembly. Visuals are produced for each focus of the week and all staff use them to stimulate discussions at appropriate opportunities. The beauty of having a mission statement that is centred on the four values of Praying, Love, Tell the Truth and Forgive, means that we are able to discuss any matters that have occurred around the world and are able to remind our children that in order to be peaceful and move past these events, we, and others, would have to embrace these four values.

Pupil voice

The School Council is an integral part of ensuring that all pupils are heard in our school. Their role has developed and they regularly meet to discuss new initiatives and make suggestions. In more recent years, they have been the glue that has fully connected the Parents' Association to the pupils. They have compiled questionnaires, met with the governing body, caterers and our local mayor. They can often be seen on Twitter, promoting upcoming events and feeding back to the school community about ongoing projects and celebration days. Pupils nominate themselves to be considered for the role and the whole school gets to vote for their chosen candidate. This process promotes democracy and aspirations. As one child said, 'I have put myself forward for the last three years and, this year, I finally got it! I persevered and it was worth it.' We have recognised the confidence that roles like these have given our pupils and the sense of ownership that they have when they know that their opinions are listened to and, where appropriate, actioned.

The School Council decided to have their own mission statement that encapsulates what they want to achieve.

School Council Mission Statement

Our role is to be the voice of the individual classes and the collective voice of the whole school.

We will work together to come up with ideas and suggestions that will enhance our school.

Our aim is to make it a happier, more interesting place to learn and offer all pupils even more opportunities than they have already.

As the voice of the school we will work with the Governors, Parents' Association and Unity Parents' Group to achieve this.

Involving our parents

Our peaceful school community is not just something that we do with our children; it also involves our parents. Our Unity Group was set up in 2014 so as to ensure that as many cultural groups as possible were represented by parents in our school in order to embrace diversity, tolerance, celebrate differences, learn about cultures/customs and raise awareness of community issues within an appropriate and proactive setting. What better place to do this than in a school?

Each parent had to write a personal statement as to why they wanted to be a member of the Unity Group in order to demonstrate their commitment to peace in our school. Members of the group work together to develop trust and understanding and to create practical opportunities to celebrate the vibrant community of our school.

In the first year of the group's existence, they created a welcoming project for the whole school. Every week, one of each of the languages spoken by the children in our school was used as the greeting of the week. This happened at the school gate, with children, parents and staff doing this in unison. What is more, the greeting was displayed around the school in communal areas and classrooms, as well as being read out over the school's public address system by a child who speaks that language at home.

Unity Coffee Mornings were held to give parents the opportunity to share traditional foods, ideas for activities throughout the academic and liturgical year, and to discuss local and international events that they may find difficult to discuss with their children. There are no topics that are off limits but we work in partnership with our parents so as to ensure that the language and any content that we use to discuss upsetting or difficult conversations are factual as well as staff-friendly, child-friendly and parent-friendly. Unity Fortnight has been the best annual celebration of cohesion that has had the biggest impact on the school community. We start and end the Unity Fortnight each year with two prayers that were written by our pupils. I am sure that anyone who had any doubts about the power of prayers could not fail to be moved by these words.

As a school, we are very proud of this group and the positive contributions that they have made, and continue to make, in our school for our pupils.

Prayers for the whole school written by the pupils

Dear Lord,

We feel so blessed to have the loving community of our school family.

Our maternal families come from all around the world and have settled here due to various life journeys, unforeseen circumstances and through choice.

We are so blessed in this school, to have a wealth of families that hold dear their beliefs, traditions and values, and that these have been passed down through generations to their children.

Wherever we originate from we are united in our faith and our love of Jesus, who has taught us to love one another, as we would like to be loved, be proud of who we are and not to judge others.

Through our faith, help us to take the time to understand and learn about others and to seek peace rather than conflict and follow in Your footsteps.

Amen

Dear Lord,

Thank you, for allowing us the time to learn and celebrate all the beautiful varieties of cultures, traditions and values that help to make our school such a special place.

We are grateful to all the people who have visited our school and shared their knowledge, personal experiences and talents to help make this fortnight interesting but also educational for us.

Our pupils and teachers have enjoyed learning things about each other's heritage that we may not have known before.

We ask You to help us to remember that, wherever we are from, we are all unique, special and loved by You.

Let our parents encourage us to respect ourselves and others around us, so that the community can be a united and welcoming place for everyone.

Amen

Our Peace Walk and safety conferences

Each year during Unity Fortnight, the children are given tasks to do at home, in school and in the local community. Our first Unity Fortnight involved the children, parents and staff doing a 'Peace Walk'. At the start of this project, Margaret Mizen (MBE) visited the school and spoke to parents about losing her son (Jimmy, at 16 years old) to mindless violence and about the importance of telling their children that they love them, that they are special and that they can do brilliant things.[1] To see so many parents crying, having been moved by Margaret's story, made the walk even more poignant.

The children had lessons about personal safety, people who make them feel safe at school and how they would like to make their community a safer place. These points were discussed as part of a School Council project that involved over ten local primary schools, and this led to over four safety conferences that were attended by local youth leaders, representatives from local councils and the Borough Commander of the Metropolitan Police.

As an end-of-project celebration, the whole school did a 'Walk for Peace'. The children made posters, banners and made up chants about peace. Parents lined up with their children and after words of encouragement from Margaret Mizen, they set off on their journey. They marched down Streatham High Road chanting, dancing and waving their messages of peace. Cars tooted their horns in support of the children and, in their words, 'It was the best day of our lives!'

As with our pupils, the Unity Parents' Group came up with their own mission statement, too. This was a powerful expression of action and passion for a school that unites in the face of changing times and does not discriminate. Every child was given a copy of this mission statement to take home and share with their families.

Unity Parents' Group Mission Statement

One religion, one God, one heart.

All united through the Catholic community of St Andrew's.

The Unity Parents' Group of St Andrew's will work together to passionately promote respect, understanding and learning together for the future of our children and the wider community.

---

1   http://forjimmy.org. Accessed 1 December 2017.

Through our parents, we will celebrate the vibrant variety of cultures in a positive and engaging way that encourages exploration rather than generalisation.

Enriching opportunities will be offered to our families to remind them that God loves all cultures, he diversified the world to make it an interesting place, and we the adults need to be both learners and educators.

Above all, we are Catholics and our actions should reflect this.

Our Year of Peace

During the second year of the Unity Group, which we called the 'Year of Peace', we arranged visits to schools of other faiths across London in order to broaden our pupils' understanding of other faiths and, more importantly, for them to see those faiths through the eyes of the children. This led to our pupils building friendships with other schools and then being invited to celebrate special religious events at those schools and being able to reciprocate these visits at our school. They were able to experience tasting celebratory foods from other cultures, looking at artefacts, and exploring similarities and differences between their faiths such as fasting, giving to charities and praying at certain times during the day. This was an enriching time for our pupils and a valuable learning journey into other faiths. One child commented, 'Wow, our faiths are almost the same, during Ramadan Muslims fast and during Lent Catholics kind of fast, too!'

Each class was given a word and they had to make a video about peace based on that word. We had a celebration assembly and the children had the exciting opportunity to view each other's videos. This was so moving and some of the children in the nursery were holding hands and hugging each other as they watched these beautiful displays of peace.

That year was also a special year for our school as we were awarded the Beacon Peaceful School Award. This recognised all the efforts that our school had made, and continues to make, in our journey for peace. Anna Lubelska, the Founder of the Peaceful Schools Movement, was one of our honorary guests at our Unity Fortnight Assembly and one of the judges, who had the difficult job of choosing a winner! It was such a special moment for our school to watch these expressions of peace and receiving the award just topped a very special celebration!

Since becoming a Beacon Peaceful School, we attended a Peaceful Schools Conference in June 2016 that was held at the beautiful historical building of Friend's House in London. The pupils who attended the conference delivered interactive workshops, participated in a panel session and joined other attendees in collective prayers and songs for peace. One pupil described it as the 'best day ever', as it celebrated all the different things that schools across the country had been doing for peace. One of the Unity Parents also attended and said that 'it was amazing to hear how powerful a child's voice can be for peace' – a message that she took back and shared with the other Unity Group members.

In December 2016, four of our School Council representatives attended a focus session to discuss what they felt individuals, schools, communities and the world could do in the future in order to spread the simple message of peace.

Building our peaceful school community throughout the year

We continue to build on our peaceful community by looking at times of the year when we remind families about focusing on peace when it can be stressful. During Advent, we get our children to discuss traditions and make Christmas decorations for our tree and we have international food events. Most year groups are involved in a nativity play and carol concert held at our local church.

One of the important things that we do during the time of remembrance is to give families the opportunity to come in to offer up prayers for loved ones who have died. We have whole school assemblies that give us the opportunity to remember those who have lost their lives during the Wars and to pray for a peaceful future. During the 'Poppies at the Tower' exhibition, our Years 5 and 6 pupils visited the Tower of London. Each child donated one pound and we bought four ceramic poppies for our school. In addition to this, every child and member of staff made a poppy and then they all walked in procession into our Remembrance Assembly and laid down their poppies. After the assembly, we recreated the 'Poppies at the Tower' in our school and encouraged our families to go and see it.

During the most holy time of Lent, we have meditations and focused prayer times and we have a Lenten challenge that involves our children doing an activity in return for sponsorship to raise money for one of the Catholic charities.

Our Years 3 and 4 pupils perform a moving and powerful Easter Reflection. This is delivered through dance, miming and freeze frames. Seeing children encapsulate the pain, discrimination and elation of the Easter story reminds us that faith and belief are not always easy journeys to undertake, but they form a foundation of who we are today.

We have many organisations, volunteers and past pupils that we invite to visit our children to deliver talks, workshops and assemblies on various safety, community and global subjects. These have included the local police, fire service, charities, food banks and local groups. We have a partnership with our local feeder school and their pupils talk to our children about their experiences of secondary school transfer, applying for jobs within their school and becoming sports leaders. Opportunities for peered learning helps our children to gain the confidence to ask questions, build relationships with local stakeholders, to be mentored by older students and acquire greater knowledge of support networks, trusted helpers and how their local community functions.

This year, we introduced 20 values that will underpin everything that we do at St Andrew's. These values were decided on and voted for by our pupils. On the last day of term, we unveiled our new values to our parents during our annual whole school parade. This took place in our playground and the route was lined by our parents. It was a fantastic finale to a busy but peace-centred year!

Concluding thoughts

Our Peaceful Community continues to grow just like our local comm-unity and the world around us. We aim to reflect what is happening around us through drama and discussion and through bringing clarity and unity through prayer, love and forgiveness.

CHAPTER 10

OUR PEACEFUL PRIMARY SCHOOL

Laura Roberts

Nothing happens unless first a dream.

Carl Sandburg (1922)[1]

Introduction

Once upon a time in the north of England, in a city called Manchester, in the area of Sale, there was a primary school called Woodheys. Imagine...

For over 20 years, as Deputy and then Headteacher, I have led Woodheys Primary School on an incredible journey of exploration, discovery and personal growth. I was continually inspired and challenged to respond to the needs of our pupils, their families and the community. One question came to me again and again over the years: What is a peaceful school? My dream and my vision were of a peaceful school in all aspects! My mission has been to create a peaceful, harmonious and successful school, where every child feels valued, safe and happy. I believe that children are our future and if we teach them well, then they will lead the way.

---

1 Carl Sandburg excerpt, 'Nothing happens unless first a dream' from the poem, 'Washington Monument By Night' from the collection, *Slabs of the Sunburnt West* (c) 1922 is reprinted by arrangement with John Steichen, Paula Steichen Polega and The Barbara Hogenson Agency, Inc. All rights reserved. For more information about Carl Sandburg, please go to www.nps.gov/carl.

All the initiatives described below support my vision to acknowledge all aspects of each child's life – addressing their needs, enhancing their intellect, developing character and uplifting their spirit. At Woodheys, we recognise that individuals learn, grow and achieve differently. Our aim is to create a safe and stimulating environment, both indoors and outdoors, where all our children feel included and valued and learn respect and tolerance for other people. We welcome all faiths and none. We are extremely proud of our diversity and our ability to work together as a TEAM: 'Together Everyone Achieves More'. Our intention is for our children to become successful global citizens of the future, who appreciate the environment and all living things.

In 2014, our school became the first ever school in the UK to be awarded Beacon Peaceful School status by Spiritual England. In June 2017, Ofsted gave us 'Outstanding' for effectiveness of leadership and management, as well as 'Outstanding' for personal development, behaviour and welfare. I am delighted to have the opportunity to share the story of how we achieved this.

How it started – reconnecting with nature

We were seeing and worrying about the increasing effects of stress on our children and their families, as well as on our staff. I began to work with psychologist Dr Jeannine Goh, Honorary Research Fellow at the University of Manchester and Associate Lecturer in Child Psychology at the Open University. We were both frustrated and sad about the society we live in. We both felt that life holds many possibilities and potentials that were not being explored and we were alarmed at the misleading messages and the increasing pressures of modern-day life. Research into the lives of young people was uncovering all-time high levels of anorexia, bulimia, self-harming and suicide as a result of a combination of academic and social media pressures. Young people who spend hours and hours on electrical devices can become detached from reality, lacking both compassion and empathy, and can become disillusioned and disenchanted, and at risk of being drawn into anti-social activities like terrorism. Jeannine started to imagine an enchanted child with all their excitement and wonder about the world, continuing to grow and develop in this way, right through to adulthood.

Jeannine and I also shared a concern that children are increasingly displaying symptoms of 'nature deprivation'. We concluded that one of the ways in which to transform this behaviour was for individuals to reconnect to themselves through time spent in nature. Jeannine has further developed this theory in her book, *The Enchanted Child*. We adopted this ethos into our Woodheys mission statement, which is summarised here as:

> Woodheys Primary School recognises each child as a unique individual – possessing talents, abilities, goals and dreams. Our mission is that we nurture each child to see themselves as an 'Enchanted Child' – a child who is delighted by the world around them. They notice, appreciate and are connected to all aspects of life. They are amazed by their bodies, which they treat with respect. They are enraptured by the power of their minds and all they can achieve. They live from their hearts and love to care and share and recognise the importance of community and working for the greater good. They look at nature with wonder and acknowledge the interconnection of everything. Excited by their own potential, they are in awe of life, the world and the universe.

We developed a big focus on environmental work that culminated in us achieving the Eco-Schools award three times. During this period, we had a vision to develop our school grounds. This was facilitated by Freda Eyden, a passionate governor who taught at our school. Freda took lessons throughout the school on sustainability and Philosophy for Children (also known as P4C).

Finding out about different faiths and beliefs

The other schools in the local area were predominantly from White British families, but our ethnic mix was increasing, which was interesting. Why? I approached some of our families of different faiths and cultures and asked why they had chosen Woodheys. I was interested in their responses. First, they said that they felt that we were very welcoming to our new families. Second, they explained that one of the principles of their faiths was to care for the environment and to be aware of sustainability issues and this resonated with what we were doing at the school.

I was inspired to find out more about different faiths and world views and pledged to visit the place of worship of every child at the school! This ignited a desire within me to develop my understanding of world faiths to a higher level, which culminated in a two-year course with the One Spirit Interfaith Foundation. I was proud to be ordained as an Interfaith Minister in July 2010. My ministry became my everyday work and as I embraced my vocation, many 'doors', began to open, along with a realisation of the interconnectedness of mankind. The course involved spiritual counselling, which addressed my own need to remain calm and centred at all times. As the Headteacher, my vision was to lead by example and practice inner peace. The skill of spiritual counselling enabled me to guide and support the community around me – the children, staff and parents.

Engaging with parents and governors

When I first began integrating interfaith and intercultural work into the school, it was to address the high-profile Government initiative at the time: 'Community Cohesion'. This meant that governors were fully behind the process. Now the Government's introduction of 'British Values' has also ensured governor backing. As parents were fully aware of our ethos from when their child started in nursery, we had little resistance. Problems did occur with families whose children began mid-year or halfway through their child's school career. For example, I had a Muslim doctor who did not want his child to learn about Christianity. I invited him in for a meeting and took him around the school to see our multicultural displays highlighting the similarities between religions and the good that is the foundation to all religions. We looked at the displays about the five pillars of Islam and the work that our children had done with our Islamic artist. I sensitively asked him how he would feel if a Christian family withdrew their child from learning about Islam. I explained that the next generation can only find peace through understanding more about other faiths and cultures. Ignorance leads to prejudice. He left after two hours of discussion, allowing his children to take part and praising our work.

Other families had concerns about their children visiting places of worship of other faiths. Where possible, I always invited these parents on our trips. Without fail it was wonderful to see the genuine interest and knowledge gained from these visits.

We host an international evening every year, where families come together as a community to share their national food and wear traditional dress where possible. Children in school learn about the different countries represented. Each year, we have well over 20 countries represented on the night. We also held international teas and coffee mornings to engage more community members. We commissioned an interfaith mural that represents children of the major faiths. The mural has information about the place of worship and the holy book used in each of the sacred spaces.

We had two Japanese families who approached me about the history of the Second World War, which was being taught to their children. There was no mention of the atomic bomb and the devastating effects on Hiroshima and Nagasaki. We decided to address this issue through the story of Sadako, the little girl who died age 12 from the effects of radiation after the bomb. Our Japanese families taught us to fold origami peace cranes. Sadako believed that if you make 1,000 paper peace cranes, then peace would come to the world. Our Japanese families have returned to Hiroshima and we have created strong links with them. We have decided to send strings of peace cranes to children in war zones around the world.

Toolkit for inner peace

I firmly believe that for the world to gain universal peace through education, everyone must be supported to find a deep level of true peace in their hearts. Our vision at Woodheys is to provide every child with a toolkit of strategies to create inner peace in their every day lives. Through yoga, mindfulness, visual meditations, breathing exercises, reflexology and peer massage, we provide experiences for children to quieten their minds, slow down and gain a level of inner peace.

During work sessions, to stimulate creativity and to calm the children's minds, members of staff have access to beautiful nature films by Mark Minard at Moving Essence. These are shown on the interactive white boards and are incredible high-quality films showing, in slow motion, wonderful landscapes, nature and moving water. As science has proved, certain frequencies of music promote calmness in children. Our corridors and Zen areas also have speakers that can broadcast this carefully selected music.

Our new building and garden

Our school intake increased from 220 to 485 over the years. In 2011, after a challenging year of redeveloping and expanding the school building to take in the higher number of pupils, we created a magnificent new building to address our vision for our children. The school was designed around a central, modern version of a 'cloisters garden', surrounded by modern classroom facilities. I wanted this area to act as a grounding point for the school. We had an allocated budget for this and an architect arrived from the local council. I proceeded to describe my vision of an area made up of several elements. I wanted a Zen garden, complete with a waterwall, a Japanese garden, a statue of a Buddha, outdoors musical instruments and wind chimes – with all the outdoor furniture built from recycled wood – and the flower beds planted with bamboos and grasses. The gentleman looked at me, didn't say a word and left. Was he in shock? However, two weeks later he reappeared with the most incredible design, bringing my vision to life. 'I've always wanted to do something like this and never had the opportunity!' he said with an enormous smile! Our children study Buddhism in Year 3 and our Zen Garden has been blessed by a Buddhist monk and Buddhist nuns.

Our Rainbow Room

As part of this new build project, we designed a beautiful and relaxing 'Rainbow Room' so that children experiencing traumatic circumstances or having anger management needs can receive support in overcoming their barriers to learning. Children in the Rainbow Room are looked after by Alison Sargent from The Hope Centre, which is also in Sale. The Rainbow Room gives children who might be worried, stressed and upset some time out so that they can calm down and have a bit of peace. Alison helps them to relax through a range of relaxation strategies and techniques that they can then use at school and at home, and this gives them the self-assurance that they can deal more calmly with difficult situations. Alison and I both believe that when children are calm and 'in the flow', then they are better able to learn and to access their own inner gifts and abilities. This project has been funded through Government pupil premium funding.

Our school grounds

Our grounds have evolved from a desert of sparse grass and tarmac to a flourishing combination of unique growing spaces. We now have five outdoor classrooms for cross-curricular work. In his film *The 11th Hour* Leonardo DeCaprio points out that 11-year-old children can identify 150 advertising logos but not the names of trees, birds or wild flowers! One of our first projects was to design a nature trail around the whole school, with colourful and well-illustrated instructional signage.

One of our legacies was to plant an Arboretum Trail of some 20 individual British specimen trees that runs around the perimeter of the school field and has a willow sculpture den for the children. Similarly, a small circular orchard of apple and pear trees was planted which has become a Sacred Grove. We have eight allotment beds built by a Community Payback team, packed with vegetables, herbs and flowers grown by our pupils. The garden shed has been painted by our pupils and representatives from the Bahá'í faith with the words, 'We are the flowers of one garden,' and, alongside this, run splayed fruit trees along the fence with the fruit at child level. Outside each classroom are planters and tubs for individual class use and these are used for gardening, science and general curriculum purposes.

With an enthusiastic and dedicated team of adults, children from all classes have enjoyed 'Planting, Picking and Tasting' sessions throughout the growing season, both in classrooms and outdoors. The eight allotment beds spring to life every March and all classes have been involved in the production of fruit, flowers and vegetables, the latter being included in delicious meals prepared by our school cook. There is even a tree nursery bed where free saplings from the Woodland Trust are developing before being found a place in the grounds. Elsewhere, tomatoes are ripening, sunflowers are heading skywards, bees are busy in the clover and the scent of the sweet peas is heavenly.

On Friday afternoons, pupils love the opportunity to participate in the Creative Nature Club, where activities so far have included making a bug camp, a bird hotel and a tepee – no wonder it's so popular! Woodcraft skills are also on offer and we have fully trained Forest School Practitioners. Recycling, waste prevention, water saving and energy conservation are also taught through all of our environmental activities, supported by our wonderful site manager.

Royal Horticultural Society (RHS) workshops, using Woodheys as a centre of excellence, have given the team lots of inspiration for year-round activities. Future plans include even more curriculum-related outdoor lessons, plus creative projects such as making new bat boxes and birdhouses. The team would also love to establish opportunities to sell produce to make their work self-sustaining.

Our labyrinth

A labyrinth is not a traditional maze. There are no tricks to it and no dead ends. A maze is designed for you to lose yourself, whereas our labyrinth is designed for you to find yourself. It has one circuitous path that meanders and winds into the centre, activating the creative side of the mind. We planted a box hedge labyrinth for peace and meditation. The labyrinth was officially opened in May 2008 with an interfaith celebration that reflected the ceremony that Pope John Paul II initiated in Assisi in 1986. Different faith leaders walked to the centre and said a prayer for global peace. At the centre of our labyrinth is a clay plaque of eight peace doves flying around the world. When the children walk the labyrinth, they experience a calming of the mind and we believe that it helps them to understand what pilgrimages are about.

The money to pay for the labyrinth actually came from funding that we received when we were awarded first prize in the country for energy conservation in the 2007 Ashden Awards. This was presented by Al Gore, former Vice President of the United States, at the Royal Geographical Society in London.

Next to the labyrinth is a special tree that children cover with colourful rainbow ribbons and prayers every year on International Peace Day (always on 21 September). As these disintegrate, they reflect the message of Buddhist prayer flags that the intentions are blown on the wind around our world. There is an artistic pottery wall plaque created by past Year 6 pupils together with the local college of art, representing all the major faith symbols, surrounded by impressions of natural elements on the left and blending into scientific symbology on the right, which illustrates the strong links within the faiths between science and nature.

We were blessed to be visited by Terry Waite, the great peace envoy. Our children were in awe of his height and his strong faith, which kept him going through adversity when he was kidnapped and held captive for four years in Lebanon. He encouraged children not to look back in anger.

Our Alex Hulme Remembrance Garden

After the death from non-Hodgkin lymphoma of a former pupil, Alex Hulme, whose brother still attended our school, we realised that lessons were to be learned in guiding children through the inevitability of loss and the circle of life. We created a sensory garden that is dedicated to Alex's memory. As a Royal Horticultural Society training school, we were asked to replicate this garden at the RHS Flower Show at Tatton Park. Colin Parry, whose son had been tragically killed in the Warrington bombings in 1993 and who has subsequently created an amazing peace centre, accompanied the school to officially open our Peace Remembrance Garden. The garden has a sensory aspect in specifically growing fragrant plants with differing textures and scents to stimulate our sense of smell. Children are encouraged to choose a special rose to plant in memory of a loved one if they suffer a loss and they also plant wooden sticks with a special memory written on them.

Other outdoor classrooms

We were able to build our Secret Garden and pond in an enclosed substantial wild garden and woodland area, as we were awarded first in the country for environmental cleanliness, and David Bellamy visited our school in person to award us our prize. This is a magical area, where children can sit and contemplate, undertake Andy Goldsworthy inspired art installations, creative writing and scientific plant and mini-beast work. We also have a large Enchanted Garden for reception and nursery children, complete with a mud kitchen, dinosaur world, rope swings, dens and a fairy grotto. All of these form part of our amazing outdoor environment, which is used regularly and enjoyed by all, contributing to whole school mental well-being and inner peace.

British values

As a peaceful school, we recognise the importance of promoting British values. The Government has a clear expectation of all schools to promote the fundamental British values of democracy, the rule of law, individual liberty, mutual respect and tolerance of those with different faiths and beliefs. At Woodheys Primary School, these values are reinforced regularly. Democracy is taught as part of the Personal,

Social, Health and Citizenship Education (PSHCE) curriculum from Years 4 to 6. The children explore the importance of the rights of adults and children, and how they have responsibilities that protect these rights. The children learn how lucky they are to live in a country with a democratic system and consider, reflect and explore what life might be like for people who do not live in a fair system. In PSHCE sessions, the children get to find out about their local MP and the different political parties. The children also enjoy taking part in role-playing a polling station activity and finding out what the voting process involves.

The rule of law and the importance of laws – whether they be those that govern the class, the school or the country – are consistently reinforced throughout regular school days, as well as when dealing with behaviour and through school assemblies. Pupils are taught the value and reasons behind laws so that they gain an understanding of how they can protect us. They also explore the responsibilities that this involves and the consequences when laws are broken. In Years 1 to 5 the children explore right and wrong through drama and role-play scenarios and find out how bad choices can affect others and the world around them. In Year 6, we explore how our country is governed and how different laws are introduced and agreed in Parliament.

Children's rights and responsibilities, as outlined by the UN Convention on the Rights of the Child, are displayed and referred to in PSHCE. Since September 2017 the new headteacher has been leading the school to become a UNICEF Rights Respecting School.

Each year, the children take part in the Crucial Crew event in Trafford, organised by the Children's Safety Education Foundation. At this event, the children meet representatives from the Fire and Police Services, Road Safety Team and School Nursing Team, and take part in activities to raise awareness of safety in the community. This also helps to heighten the respect and value of local services.

Individual liberty is taught at the school, and pupils are actively encouraged to make choices, knowing that they are in a safe and supportive environment. Pupils are encouraged to know, understand and exercise their rights and personal freedoms, and we advise them how to exercise these safely, for example through our E-Safety and PSHCE lessons. Mutual respect is part of our school's ethos. Our behaviour policy has revolved around core values, such as respect, and pupils have been part of discussions and assemblies related to what this means and how it is shown. Posters around the school promote respect for others and this is reiterated through our classroom and learning rules, as well as our behaviour policy.

Tolerance of those of different faiths and beliefs is achieved through enhancing the pupils' understanding of their place in a culturally diverse society and by giving them opportunities to experience such diversity. Lessons and discussions involving prejudices and prejudice-based bullying have been followed and supported by learning in RE, the Peace Mala Project and PSHCE. Woodheys is the Trafford RE hub school and hosts meetings and training for Trafford teachers. All UK schools need to follow a 'broadly based Christian' agenda, balanced with positive information about the other major faiths, including Islam, Judaism, Buddhism, Hinduism and Sikhism. I was involved in the development of the last two RE curriculums for Trafford schools.

In Year 5, our pupils are introduced to Humanism. The message is: 'You don't have to have God to be good!' We do have a school prayer in assembly and at lunchtime. Our lunchtime organiser is a Muslim lady, and she ensures that no child is forced to say prayers but can just bow their head in respect. Children learn the National Anthem and are shown 'The Lord's Prayer' as a UK tradition.

At each peace event, we send home postcards of a Global Peace Prayer created by Vanessa Edwards. There are over 200,000 postcards flying around our world and it is known that they have visited at least 130 countries. This encourages the children to understand the use and power of positive language, words and phrasing.

Woodheys was awarded the Religious Education Quality Mark Gold in 2016.

Peace Mala

We are a Peace Mala Gold accredited school. The Peace Mala Project represents faith, culture, gender, disability and is non-political. The theme that underpins the Peace Mala scheme runs through all the major faiths and is called the 'Golden Rule' – 'Do unto others as you would have done to you.' This interfaith project was created by Pam Evans after the terrorist attacks in the United States on 11 September 2001. The Peace Mala message is symbolised by a double-rainbow bracelet, with the colours representing different religions. The central white bead is 'you', even if you don't have a faith. There is also a clear bead that brings everything together and represents peace and harmony. Pam Evans explains:

> Peace education is more important than ever with the current world climate of fear and misunderstanding. Extremism flourishes wherever reason is suppressed and freedom of thought and speech is discouraged. Interfaith dialogue for peace is vital in the education of our children. This is where the Peace Mala project has so much to offer as it introduces children and young people to the Golden Rule that exists in all religions, spiritual paths and cultures.

Our Afritwin Project

Woodheys' international links have always been strongest with South Africa, with our Afritwin Project. Through British Council funding, we were able to link with schools in Durban and Cape Town. I was honoured to be invited by Archbishop Desmond Tutu to walk the labyrinth at St George's Cathedral in Cape Town and then take communion from him. We gifted the Archbishop a Peace Mala bracelet, which he supports wholeheartedly as he created the phrase 'The Rainbow Nation' about the people of South Africa. Our teachers visited our link schools and we hosted the African teachers. During one of the visits, we linked with the organisation 'May Peace Prevail on Earth' and commissioned a Peace Pole to be planted in our Zen area.

Unity in the face of adversity

Schools are increasingly having to cope with the effects of Government legislation, bureaucracy and critical incidents. The effect on schools after the Brexit vote in 2016 and the traumatic Manchester bombing in 2017 are real-life scenarios that, as a headteacher, I have had to respond to and help keep our community balanced. I have realised how developing a peaceful school has prepared us and our community to maintain our incredible unity in the face of adversity.

We were all shocked by the tragic bombing of the Ariana Grande concert at the Manchester Evening News Arena on the evening of 22 May 2017. Our school community joined together in condemnation of the action and in sending our love and condolences to all the families affected. Throughout the week, we updated our families with any information from our local authority that could help parents to explain to their children and support them in the following weeks. Staff sensitively addressed issues when they arose with our children. As the Islamic period of Ramadan began the following weekend, we had already booked Razwan Ul-Haq, an Islamic artist, to work with our Year 5. After consultation, we decided to go ahead with this as Razwan had worked with us many times and is a wonderfully compassionate man, who joined the world in condemning the action of the perpetrator.

In reaction to the event, we also created a multifaith assembly, focusing on the unity and peace between us all. The three Abrahamic religions – Judaism, Christianity and Islam – were represented. We told the children about the significance of a flag flying at half mast and that we observed a minute's silence at 11 a.m. in remembrance of the victims and their families. Our non-uniform day supported the Manchester appeal for the families and survivors of the terrorist attack. All our children, took home Vanessa Edward's 'Prayer for Global Peace' and Key Stage 2 children were given some sweets by our Muslim children, who took them around the classrooms.

On 21 June 2017, we were joined by many faith representatives, and also by the Mayor of Trafford Councillor Jonathan Coupe, to celebrate the Peace Mala Gold Award ceremony. There were around 300 children in the assembly hall, who sang the very moving song 'I am the Earth'. They had been designated a non-uniform day and asked to wear a colour of the rainbow, depending on their year group, the eldest wearing red, going through orange, yellow, green and blue. The nursery children were wearing indigo and violet and joined us in the playground for the whole school to unite after assembly. We created a giant rainbow in the playground and reflected that the rainbow is the symbol of peace and hope for the future. We all joined together to sing Ariana Grande's song for the 'One Love' Manchester memorial concert, 'Somewhere Over the Rainbow'. The children ended by forming a beautiful heart symbol with their hands.

A blueprint for Peaceful Schools

I retired in July 2017, and am delighted to have left this Peaceful School legacy, which has recently been recognised by Ofsted during June 2017, when we gained Outstanding in effectiveness of leadership and management and personal development, behaviour and welfare.

Below are some of the Ofsted report comments, which confirm the success of our vision to be a 'blueprint' for peaceful primary schools:

- Woodheys School provides an oasis of calm tranquility for parents, staff and pupils. They are all extremely proud of their school. Parents say the school wholeheartedly celebrates the diversity of the community.

- Inclusion, British values, social, spiritual and moral messages are interwoven into the curriculum so that pupils celebrate difference.

- Leaders ensure that they offer a holistic approach to pupils and their families. The 'Zen Garden', the 'Labyrinth', the 'Rainbow Room' and the Early Years 'Secret Garden' all provide peaceful spaces for reflection.

- Teachers and leaders work with local clusters of schools and have joined the local teaching school alliance. They work with the local authority and other schools to share good practice and lead the religious education hub for the local authority.

- Staff morale is high and all the staff feel passionate about the school's vision that 'Together Everyone Achieves More'.

- Leaders ensure that the spiritual, moral, social and cultural development of the pupils is delivered through the 'Junior Peace Mala', interfaith and community cohesion work. The Afritwin Project provides a further dimension for pupils to develop their understanding of another culture. This approach places the Woodheys School at the heart of their multicultural community.

- Pupils are taught to be tolerant, respectful young people. They understand the true meaning of 'difference' and show genuine respect towards other people.

- British values are taught well and embedded across the school. Pupils understand the concept of democracy introduced to them through the school council system, and recognise the value of being able to contribute to decision-making processes. Leaders recognise that in creating a harmonious, tolerant community they are preparing pupils for life beyond the confines of the school.

- The school's work to promote pupils' personal development and welfare is outstanding.

- Adults and pupils share a culture of mutual respect and care. Pupils are very considerate to each other and celebrate any differences. Inspectors saw many examples of cooperation in lessons and during social times.

- Pupils say that they feel safe in school. This view is positively reinforced by staff and parents. Pupils report that instances of bullying are very rare in the school, and are confident that they would be dealt with effectively by staff. All pupils feel supported by staff and know who they can turn to if they have any concerns.

- Pupils know how to stay safe online and personally as a result of the high-quality teaching they receive. Parents have attended sessions on online safety and governors are keenly aware of their duties and responsibilities in this area.

- Pupils are given a true sense of identity where differences are celebrated. They understand the diverse cultures and faiths that make up the community and their roles within it.

- The behaviour of pupils is outstanding.

- Pupils are tolerant and embrace others' views. As one pupil expressed, 'No one makes fun of differences here.' Pupils greeted inspectors with warmth and welcomed them into the school. All adults in the school are excellent role models for pupils.

- Without exception, the parents state that their children enjoy coming to school. As a result attendance is high.

- The nurturing environment means children are safe and thoroughly enjoy their time in the Nursery and Reception provisions. There is an attractive outdoor area with a charming Secret Garden that provides a cosy corner for the children.

- Parents are united in their love of the school: 'My daughter has come on in leaps and bounds since starting at Woodheys. I have only had positive experiences with this school and the teachers.'

Concluding thoughts

At Woodheys we live our values. Happiness is proven to be linked to caring, charity and contributing. Sadly, children who only focus on material issues and only want to achieve monetary wealth in life do not achieve the happiness linked to those who aspire to help others. Education needs to develop active, compassionate and lifelong learners who understand that other people, with their differences, can be heard. As teachers, we embrace the heliotropic effect and our children, as the flowers, will follow the light. All living systems grow towards the light, and are attracted to that which is light. We are a school emanating love and light.

Further reading

Goh, J. and Owen, S. (2014) *The Enchanted Child*. Manchester: Awespace.

Twyman, J.F. (2000) *Praying Peace*. Forres: Findhorn Press.

Weil, P. (1990) *The Art of Living in Peace*. Accessed 1 December 2017 at http://unesdoc. unesco.org/images/0008/000886/088669eb.pdf.

Organisations and websites

Afritwin Project – www.afritwin.net

Alex Hulme Foundation – www.alexhulmefoundation.co.uk

Dr Masaru Emote – www.masaru-emoto.net/english/water-crystal.html

Global Peace Prayer created by Vanessa Edwards – www.vandaehworks.co.uk

Interfaith Foundation – www.interfaithfoundation.org

Labyrinth Society – www.labyrinthsociety.org

Mark Minard at Moving Essence – www.movingessence.net

Peace Mala – www.peacemala.org.uk

Razwan Ul Haq – www.ulhaq.com

RE Today – www.retoday.org.uk

REQM – www.reqm.org

Spiritual England – www.spiritualengland.org.uk

Teaching Citizenship – www.teachingcitizenship.org.uk

The Monastery – www.themonastery.co.uk

UNICEF – www.unicef.org.uk

veriditas – www.veriditas.org

Woodheys Primary School – www.woodheysprimaryschool.co.uk

Woodheys Primary School 80 Anniversary film – www.youtube.com/watch?v=EH6lfC mzAC8&feature=youtu.be

World Peace Prayer Society (May Peace Prevail On Earth) – www.worldpeace.org

CHAPTER 11

OUR PEACEFUL SECONDARY SCHOOL

Cardinal Newman Catholic School Coventry

Introduction

Cardinal Newman Catholic School is one of three Catholic secondary schools in Coventry serving the Catholic community in the north-west of the city. Cardinal Newman has over 1,270 students, including over 200 students in the sixth form. Our city is recognised as a symbol of world peace and reconciliation following the devastation caused by the heavy bombing of the Second World War. We believe that it is essential that our students understand what this means, and how they have an essential role to play in incorporating the message of peace and reconciliation in the everyday things that they do.

Cardinal Newman's mission statement, 'Knowledge through the light of faith,' has proved a firm foundation for learning, questioning how we can share the Gospel values. The need to give a voice to every member of the community, and take time to listen, instigated a review of the values that would enable everyone to use their gifts and talents and be the best person they can be. Students, staff, parents and governors came together to establish that the motto, 'Aspire to inspire,' would highlight the qualities needed to grow as fulfilled members of the school community. Taking the five letters of ASPIRE, we agreed that it would mean: Achievement, Service, Peace, Integrity, Respect and Excellence. The very essence of working together needs a real understanding of peace at our core as we can often be reminded by Blessed John Henry Newman's words, 'Heart speaks unto heart.'

Therefore, building that peaceful environment has to be rooted in modelling positive behaviour and having a pastoral system that can skillfully use restorative justice when we need to repair behaviour that has fallen short of our expectations. The language used on a daily basis underpins positive behaviour and is continually echoed in the school's Rewards Policy.

This chapter is about the journey that we have been on to become the first secondary school in the country to be awarded Beacon Peaceful School status. It includes a contribution from Dennis Davison, a Normandy Landings veteran of the Second World War, who has played an instrumental role by sharing his stories with our students and teaching them the value of learning from past conflicts in order to create a more peaceful and secure future.

The beginnings

Our journey began in the school year 2013/2014, while working on a city project called 'Peace through Unity', organised by the local charity Normandy Day UK, to commemorate the seventieth anniversary of the D-Day Landings. Rhys Davies, Head of Humanities at Cardinal Newman, was instrumental in leading this project and has worked tirelessly on developing the theme within our school community. The project involved our students meeting and working with D-Day veterans and other veterans of the Second World War so as to learn about D-Day and their individual experiences of conflict. The students interviewed the veterans and valued how they shared their memories with them. The students produced a peace banner and video, demonstrating the importance of this event.

What was apparent from the start of the project was that this was not just a History project about the D-Day Landings but a project linking different generations for the sole purpose of passing on the baton of peace. The idea was initiated by the founder of Normandy Day UK, Dennis Davison. The aim of the project for him was to ensure that young people found out about the horrors of D-Day and of war in general. Dennis hoped that, as a result, students would carry that baton of peace, acting as peace ambassadors and peaceful citizens. Dennis was eager to explain that he did not want young people to witness or experience the horrors of war. The project really started something special in our school and the idea of being a peaceful school was born.

Peace through unity

The curriculum has provided a great means for staff to engage our students in understanding how they can become active responsible citizens and contribute to creating a peaceful world. This has been harnessed enthusiastically by the History Department, which channels the students' natural inquisitive nature to consider past historical conflicts and how peace and reconciliation can emerge through the endeavours of remarkable individuals. Students look at role models, such as Martin Luther King or Mother Theresa, to explore how they used diplomatic skills and strategies and are challenged to consider their own peacemaking skills. Always looking for ways to collaborate in practical activities, it was not surprising that the History Department responded to the invitation to join the citywide 'Peace through Unity' project. They welcomed the opportunity for a group of students to meet the personnel from the Normandy Landings in their research to understand the Second World War.

Dennis Davison

The school has forged a very special relationship with Dennis Davison, a British D-Day veteran recognised by both the British Empire Medal and by France's highest award, the Légion d'honneur, for his distinguished service during the D-Day Landings and the Allied invasion of mainland Europe. His story has captivated the students, who enjoy his visits and participation in school events. They shared with him the creative plans for a large peace banner, which now serves as a backdrop adjacent to our Peace Garden. The Peace Garden was built following the project and is a haven of tranquility on a very busy school site. It is a place that celebrates the memories of deceased students and staff, as well as the focus for Armistice Day in November. Students tend the area and have made their own ceramic poppies to display. The legacy of the peace project in 2014 is the way in which students and staff work in partnership with Dennis to spread peace and reconciliation through positive action. 'Somehow, I just feel in tune with the school,' he says. 'They are doing a wonderful job.' The following is Dennis's message to all young people:

> The D-Day Landings were the turning point in World War 2. The price was high, but the consequence of failure could not be

contemplated. We must never forget the sacrifices made by our Armed Forces, both then and now, in protecting our security, freedoms and democracy. Most of the Western world has now enjoyed relative peace and security since 1945. That gives me hope that, by seeking to understand others and embracing our differences, armed conflict can be avoided. Long after I'm gone, I hope Normandy Day UK continues to bring people from across the generations and nations together in schools and local communities to protect the legacy of D-Day in perpetuity and promote peace and understanding between people of all backgrounds, religions and cultures.

Cardinal Newman has always had a peaceful atmosphere thanks to its Catholic ethos and as a result of the work that students and staff undertake for local, national and international charities. However, it was as a result of the 'Peace through Unity' project that the school community started to look at peace as something that had to be learned about and acted upon and not just something that could be taken for granted. Students, with the support of staff, started to realise that peace can easily disappear if it is not acknowledged and this can happen not just on a global scale with conflicts around the world but also on a smaller scale with family, friends and themselves.

Through the project and the work of Dennis, we formed our Peace and Justice Group. Students worked to spread the message of peace across the school. The group led on other projects, including Legacy 110, a nationwide project commemorating the centenary of the First World War. As a result of the Legacy 110 project, students had the opportunity to visit the First World War battlefields and the school created the Peace Garden. As already mentioned, this is where the peace banner hangs, acting as a lasting memorial to those who sacrificed their lives for peace in our world.

Other peace projects

As a Catholic school, we have an active chaplaincy team led by a full-time lay chaplain. Every day begins and ends with a prayer. Pope Francis reminds us, 'Let us pray for peace and let us bring it about, starting in our own homes!' The opportunity to offer prayer intentions is intrinsic in all our liturgical celebrations throughout the year and in weekly Masses and assemblies. The chapel and Peace

Garden prove inspirational places for reflection, exploring one's spirituality, reconciliation meetings or just being oneself. The students also feel the call to respond with prayer to issues that they face in their daily lives or to comprehend global events that challenge world peace. Nurturing this prayer life is key to providing holistic care to each member of the community.

A recent school retreat day was dedicated to the concept of peace. The students spent time off-timetable, working with tutors to reflect upon inner peace, peace in the community and peace in the wider world. In their exploration, students considered how they could promote and become active peacemakers. The sessions provided students with the opportunity for discussion and creative expression, concluding with a very powerful whole school peace protest.

The Spectrum Support Programme (a branch of Rainbows Bereavement Support) offered to our students is another means of learning about self and inner peace, especially for those students who have a troubled life at home. It supports those students who have suffered some form of grief – a bereavement, a family separation, family difficulties or any form of change that has brought about a sense of loss.

Other projects that the students' Peace and Justice Group has overseen include: Holocaust Memorial Day, Send My Friend to School, organising a Peace Day on the seventy-fifth anniversary of the Coventry Blitz, working with Coventry Migrant and Refugee Centre and also implementing the school's first ever Peace Charter.

Antony Owen, peace poet

Many more enrichment ideas have developed our commitment to being a Beacon School of Peace, which has been described in detail by our visiting peace poet, Antony Owen. Antony writes:

> I am writing to your school to convey my admiration and respect regarding the multitude of peace education activities you engage in. These are tumultuous times so peace education is never more important. When I visited schools in Hiroshima last year I was heartened to see that peace education is a mandatory inclusion to the curriculum. As Coventry is also a city of peace and reconciliation largely connected to our Cathedral it is important local schools make

every effort to include peace education where they can. I feel that Cardinal Newman Catholic School is an exceptional school that sets, not just follows, examples of peace education for other schools to follow. Time and time again I have seen the positive life-affirming impact it has had on your students, from the CND Peace Education assembly to the Hiroshima and Coventry Blitz workshops that I presented. Looking through some of the one hundred or so poems your students wrote I feel that peace education is not only working but inspiring students to see poetry and language far beyond the parameters of the curriculum. In years to come, future students will look back on what your students and teachers have done today and feel very proud of the proactive stance you have made. Well done to all of you and I leave you with a very poignant poem that one of your fantastic students, Molly Higgins, wrote on 13 Nov 2014 for the Coventry Blitz memorial.

MY ONLY CRIME
by Molly Higgins
(Year 10, Cardinal Newman Catholic School)

As I rise from the shadows on the ground
I see what I can only guess is my shadow,
but she is nowhere to be seen, in-fact I can't see anyone but I can see —
Shadows,
I see my own shadow but it won't move, it is forever imprinted on a pavement.
I know now I'm dead, a ghost of my former self,
I never got to have a boyfriend, a child.
I know who did this
But what did I do?
I am innocent —
My only crime was being,
In Hiroshima.

Cardinal Newman Catholic School Peace Charter

When we were awarded the Beacon Peace School status, the work of being a Peace School had only just begun. Through our pastoral sessions, we considered the impact of this accolade and its implications for the school community. We looked at the four levels of peace and reflected on what we had already achieved for ourselves and for the school. Students were asked to think of the barriers that could occur in stopping them in achieving the different levels of peace and what could be done to overcome them. They also made personal pledges on how they would strive to achieve inner peace. From this body of works, our whole school Peace Charter was created. It outlines the rationale for our work on peace within ourselves, the school, local area and global community. It was written by our students, who are committed to ensuring that we try every day to achieve the Peace Charter's goals. It symbolises our continuous journey and recognises that the whole community has a contribution to make.

Peace Charter
Inner peace for the individual student and member of staff

- We will take time each day to pray.

- We will treat others as we would like to be treated.

- We will always try to forgive others.

- We will be kind with the words we use.

- We will take time to listen to each other.

- We will provide a place of sanctuary where students are able to reflect and be calm.

Peaceful relationships and constructive resolution of conflicts

- We will follow the school code of conduct at all times.

- We will look out for members of our school who are unhappy.

- We will report any problems that we or our friends are having.

- We will try not to judge others for their actions or words.

- We will have clear fair and consistent sanctions for all.

- We will strive for peaceful resolution of conflicts.

- We will learn how to reduce conflict in peer groups.

Peaceful school ethos and environment

- We will put our litter in the bin and encourage others to do so.

- We will respect the school environment in classrooms and around the school.

- We will support members of our school community at social times in school.

- We will show good manners to all by doing some of the following: opening the door for others, saying 'please' and 'thank you', not jumping the dinner queue, giving up our seat on the bus for a member of the public.

Peacemaking within the wider community and world

- We will contribute to the charity life of the school throughout the year.

- We will try to take on any opportunity to support others in our local community.

- We will volunteer at least once a year to help others in our school or community.

- We will show respect to our local community on the way to and from school.

- We will think of others before we think of ourselves.

Concluding comments

Cardinal Newman Catholic School understands the responsibility of ensuring that our whole school community is aware of the importance of being people of peace in a troubled world. The Second World War veteran, Dennis Davison, who has been inspirational, saw this in his vision for his project and we see this in our vision for our school community. We are so familiar with Blessed John Henry Newman's prayer, which reminds us of how we have been created to do some definite service and are a link in a chain, a bond of connection between persons. We see how significant that reflection is as we continue our peace journey. Our message is powerful: 'Peace – pass it on!'

CHAPTER 12

OUR PEACEFUL SPECIAL SCHOOL

Moira Thompson

Introduction

This is our school,
Let peace live here,
Let the rooms be full of happiness,
Let love be all around...

So begins our school prayer! Every time I hear the children say and sign this prayer I feel a real tingle and I think: 'Yes, this really is our school and peace is at the heart of Hawthorns.' Saying and signing this prayer together each Friday during our Achievers' Assembly is a very strong school ritual. Hawthorns School is, in every sense of the word, special. We are a Primary Special School and we meet the requirements of learners who have a wide range of complex needs. The children who attend our school are aged between 5 and 11 years and they are mainly from the Tameside area, East Manchester, with a few children from neighbouring authorities. The children arrive at different ages and stages of their primary education – this is due to the nature of their needs and when the children are assessed for an Education Health and Care plan.

I have been a teacher, deputy, headteacher and now Executive Principal of this wonderful school for 35 years. During all my time here, I have hoped to make a difference to the lives of everyone who comes here – children, staff and parents. My aim has always been to lead a school where children are happy, safe and successful and, of course, peaceful. I wanted to nurture peace and love amongst all our school community to make sure that we treated each human being with love, care and respect. This is a principle that sits at the heart of all that I do.

In my own life as a pupil, student teacher and teacher I have felt a strong desire to ensure that everyone feels valued, respected and supported, no matter what their abilities, and that they feel and experience real peace and love. So, what do I mean by that?

For me, peace is a state of harmony, characterised by a lack of violence and any other types of conflict behaviours, as well as freedom from the fear of violence. What is more, peace also suggests to me the existence of healthy or newly healed interpersonal relationships, the establishment of equality and a working order that serves the true interests of all. Therefore, this is what we at Hawthorns work hard to create and sustain within the school. We also help the children develop an understanding and experience of what it is to be a peaceful individual. Given the nature of our children's learning needs, this requires a systematic, supportive and planned whole school programme that can introduce, develop and embed these peaceful principles.

This is so important to me. As a child in primary school, from time to time, I witnessed adult behaviour that made me feel so anxious, and, on some occasions, I even saw extreme aggression from teachers. I saw teachers who were unable to cope with learners who were challenging. Even though I did not fall foul of their ways or expectations myself, I saw other children, mostly boys, beaten and smacked and shouted at for being unable to complete tasks or conform. This filled me with dreadful fear and horrible apprehension at what would happen if someone stepped out of line. I remember wanting desperately to teach but knowing that the children in my classroom would never feel such fear or anxiety. The thumping heartbeat, hot sweaty palms, lump in throat and holding back tears was something I would never inflict on another soul. As a mother and grandmother, too, I would never want my children to experience that fear. The principle of peace is therefore one that I work hard to cultivate.

Why is peace so important?

As my teaching career began, I still witnessed practice that I regarded as unsavoury in terms of how adults spoke to children, how they modelled behaviour, responses and reactions and how some professionals treated children, parents and other adults. But, on the other hand, I saw the impact that kindness and compassion can have on children and I saw how these attributes could create a place of peace, a place of sanctuary. In my view, this popular saying emphasises a key concept: 'People will forget what you did but they will never forget how you made them feel.' Each one of us, I am sure, can recollect that teacher or adult who made us feel safe, supported and valued.

The reality of our time is that we all suffer stress and anxiety. That is part of being human and also the stressful times we live in. The most important climate we can create in school is to make it into a place where peace sits at the heart of all we do. I believe that as school leaders, we need to convey our aspirations to others and create the kind of culture, where emotional development and intelligence are nurtured. Within this culture we then need to develop practice that supports the management of emotions, feelings and stress.

At Hawthorns, our learners' needs are complex and diverse and we recognise that many of our learners, especially those children diagnosed with autism, experience heightened levels of stress and anxiety from the moment they wake until they go to sleep. Whereas around one in ten of the general population may be suffering from anxiety, for children and adults diagnosed with Autism Spectrum Condition (ASC), Attention Deficit Hyperactivity Disorder (ADHD) and other learning needs, there is a much higher percentage suffering from anxiety.

Many of the children at Hawthorns also have sensory issues, which means that they are over-sensitive or under-sensitive to some kinds of sensory input. Sensory input is anything that our senses interpret that may be through any of our senses: sight, sound, smell, touch, taste, proprioception and vestibular. Our proprioception sense means being aware of our bodies and knowing where we are in space. Our vestibular sense helps us to understand our body and how we move and balance. Sensory issues may mean that a child is over-sensitive to things around them such as sounds or smells and bright lights. When our children experience sensory problems, they are unable to interpret information from these senses and this can, and does, increase stress that can manifest in many ways.

A planned curriculum for peace

My experience has taught me the importance of consistency and the importance of training staff to understand why and how to create calm teaching contexts. We teach staff that all adults can support children confidently and can model positive behaviours. In 2008, as we recognised the importance of having a planned curriculum to develop emotional intelligence and peacefulness, we needed to decide on how to deliver provision that recognised the importance of children being ready to learn as well as being able to support their anxieties. I knew that we needed a cohesive, consistent way of ensuring that we were able to develop each child's emotional intelligence and thus focus on peace in our school.

The timing was critical as we were at the point of moving to a new co-located campus and we needed to consider how we could use a sensory room to best effect for our children. So, the quest was on! Some members of staff were charged with looking at different programmes and strategies. I knew that we had found the answer when two members of staff talked about A Quiet Place (AQP).

A Quiet Place (AQP)

A Quiet Place[1] was developed by Penny Moon and it is not just a space, a place, a room or a cosy environment. It is so much more. AQP is a concept, essentially a state of mind. It is how to achieve this peaceful state of mind that is the key to any personal development work. All who have worked with children have many times told them to be calm, but some children simply do not know how to be clam. 'Telling' is simply not good enough – showing and experiencing are the best ways of learning with many of our Hawthorns pupils. AQP offers a myriad of ways, using differentiated learning styles so that all can begin to understand the physiology of emotion and have techniques to help them harness emotion positively and manage their lives better.

The underlying assumptions of AQP are that everyone has a wealth of, as yet untapped, potential and if our techniques can empower the individual to become aware of this and begin to tap into this inner wealth, then they will be better able to become the best they can be.

---

1   www.aquietplace.co.uk. Accessed 2 December 2017.

To this end, AQP offers individual and group programmes that can be personalised for all ages and abilities. The programmes are holistic and educational in their approach, with a therapeutic underpinning. AQP uses a triangulated evidence-based approach, supporting the achievement of unique outcomes derived from three key stakeholders: the child, the parent and the member of staff. AQP promotes and demonstrates improvements in:

- emotional intelligence
- well-being/stress levels
- resilience and empathy
- body language/non-verbal communication
- academic performance and motivation.

The AQP programmes of well-being for pupils, families and staff, as well as classroom programmes like Ready Steady Learn and Peer Massage in class, offer a breadth of inclusive provision designed to make the whole school a calmer place, where peace is more likely to flourish with everyone feeling safer, better and more in control of themselves.

Originally, the AQP programmes were designed to offer effective interventions within a half-term timetable; Penny Moon's key principles were to avoid the disruption of peripatetic services popping in and out as well as avoiding children feeling stigmatised. Penny wanted to see rapid and effective change, using this non-stigmatised personal development educational approach. It avoided the sense of children being 'sent' to see someone as if something was wrong with them. I was attracted even more to AQP as a member of our staff team would be able to deliver the programmes. I love the name 'A Quiet Place' because it reflects the outcomes of the programmes. There is a real connection to that place of peace, spirit and love that is deep in our hearts.

AQP may also include an environment with very specific aims that will enhance the delivery of AQP programmes. This is not like any of the usual environments placed in schools such as chill-out rooms for behaviour management or multisensory rooms that are essentially designed to stimulate. Nor is it a total immersion room, where images are projected onto surrounding walls of various environments in order to assist the development of creative writing skills and other areas of learning across the curriculum. AQP is a healing environment, a consistent place of peace with a little twinkle, a treasure house for anyone, with a gentle atmosphere that reminds some adults of being in church. Our children tend to whisper when they go in. It is a place of awe and wonder for them, and a place where it is safe to relax and be themselves. It has been described scientifically as a place to enhance theta rhythms in the brain. Theta brain waves make us feel calm and at peace and help the learning process.

A Quiet Place at Hawthorns

AQP was introduced into Hawthorns carefully. A planned programme was designed to ensure that the whole staff team understood AQP principles. We spoke to our school governors and to parents.

Without full staff commitment and understanding, I did not believe that it would work successfully. Having introduced the concept, the principles and the way in which AQP might work, we set about designing the environment and staff began training. Some staff went on the Educational Therapeutics Programme and some staff began the AQP Facilitator Programme.

The commitment is a challenge in terms of staff time and the need to have ongoing training, but it is essential if the AQP magic is to work.

A carefully planned introduction and training plan was planned with the AQP team. We began by ensuring that we had:

- two AQP champions on the Speech and Language Team

- one fully trained facilitator

- one body worker for massage

- all children able to access the resource on a rolling programme

- some children who would have the six weeks 'protocol' (i.e. the special programme)

- staff introduced to classroom relaxation techniques, HeartMath and Peer Massage

- staff training that underpinned the introduction and continues to be an ongoing development programme

- ongoing development for parents and families.

The 'protocol' programme of six weeks offers individualised sessions to children, which includes taught timetabled activities, play, stories and relaxation as well as visualisation. A body worker also offers hand or foot massage and the children also access the HeartMath programme. The children on protocol can be offered up to 90 minutes across the week, however, for our children, it is tailored to meet their needs. Throughout the sessions, there is a focus on the present and on dreams and aspirations. There are targeted outcomes from all participants, the pupil, parent/carer and teacher.

The support from Penny Moon and her AQP team was excellent and just as a tree begins its life as a tiny seedling, and then the roots grow and slowly the tree begins to take form, so did AQP grow and develop at Hawthorns.

What do our children, staff and parents say about AQP?

So, what do the staff and children say? Sparkling moments are captured and these are the times when you know that something special has happened.

Children have said:

'I like AQP – it is fun and there is peace and quiet.'

'AQP makes me feel happy, it is calm and cosy.'

'It is a good idea to practice my breathing before my football tournament, I don't want a yellow card.'

'When you do your magic button, it's magic and you feel happy all day.'

'That was amazing!' (upon returning from an AQP session)

'I breathe slowly to let the calm in.'

'I have my calm back, it felt like I was in the story, I could feel the warmth of the beach.'

'I am multicoloured with happiness.'

'When I relax in the chair it makes me feel soft and warm in my heart.'

Parents have said:

> 'AQP feels like home even though it doesn't have a kitchen.'

> 'I'm amazed, he has shown me how to do calm breathing; he is managing his frustrations much more.'

> 'He has apologised for his behaviour as a result of having an AQP session.'

> 'I've seen her walk away from volatile situations and cool off since she has been to AQP.'

Staff members have said:

> 'He takes himself away and calms down using the magic button.'

> 'She shares her anxieties instead of running off or hitting out.'

> 'He is much happier communicating feelings; he is able to stop and think before reacting.'

> 'Following Session 2 of the Magic Carpet, we have seen an amazing change in this anxious child, he is now able to calm and relax so quickly.'

Ensuring AQP works well

One of the key elements that ensures that our AQP is successful is the skilled Facilitator. Our Facilitator has been trained and receives high-quality professional supervision from the AQP organisation. Our Facilitator ensures that our protocol children have high-quality, memorable learning experiences. The body worker works seamlessly within the programme and provides massage that the children relish!

The Facilitator records key observations

Here are some examples of the Facilitator's recorded observations:

- When benchmarking a boy aged nine, he said that he was feeling happy because his Mum and Dad are happy. They are happy because he is behaving at school and getting 'Green'.

- 'Green makes you calm' (HeartMath). He also likes to choose a green smelly tissue for calm breathing!

- Target set by parent 'to be kinder to siblings'. When benchmarking at the end of sessions child said the little boy in the tree was happy because he was being kind.

- A child aged six had an agreed target to share and be gentler when playing with siblings. Parents are much happier with the child's listening skills. The child is responding much more at home and also communicating more about his school day.

- Parents were pleasantly surprised at how much their child was enjoying drawing and painting in AQP. They are going to try some massage at home too!

- More members of staff are requesting revisits for children who have already been through the AQP programme due to emotional difficulties/behaviour and changes or concerns from home.

- When doing Personal, Social and Health Education…a boy who had been on the protocol and having some behaviour issues…the class learning objective was 'to recognise and deal with feelings of anger' and the boy said 'I calm down by breathing slowly. And I move away and use the magic button.'

- 'Mummy helps me with my breathing and it helps me to feel calm.'

- A support staff member was really amazed when she prompted an anxious child to use their magic button and she has successfully used this technique to help the child to manage stress and calm down discreetly. They were both calmer and the situation was resolved much more quickly.

Benefits and challenges

I am delighted that we made the decision to embrace A Quiet Place and ensure that it sits at the heart of our school. Each year, AQP provides a report that collates all the evidence and interprets the overall findings.

The report details how many pupils have been on the protocol and how many AQP sessions have been delivered through the year.

We receive a breakdown of improvement scores in Academic Performance, Motivation and Reduction of Stress levels in pupils and staff. The report records how many pupils use techniques to calm themselves down. It records improvements in body language.

The report identifies which areas of emotional intelligence were focused on most – often, this is managing feelings followed by communication and self-awareness. The report then summarises the improvements in emotional intelligence. The report gives the reader a real flavour of the impact on children, how wonderful to hear AQP described as: 'Refreshing and delicious – when there is trouble I walk away.'

The reports include comments from parents. For example, a parent told a member of staff that their child was having a troubled morning. The parent then decided to play 'fairy ring'. That did the trick. The pupil arrived at school calm and ready to learn.

Hawthorns continues to be a calm school, where children's emotional development has a high priority, however there are challenges. The children who come to Hawthorns have increasing complexity in terms of their cognition and learning; communication and interaction; physical and sensory needs and their social and mental health needs. Therefore, there is a need to adapt AQP in order that it reaches and meets the needs of all of our learners.

Working with children who are very young in age and whose emotional development is still at an early stage means that results are not always seen immediately. But the key is patience, consistency and continuity. We believe that the practice will have a beneficial impact and positive outcomes.

The challenge of working with parents who do not value the techniques mean that, unfortunately, some children are unable to practise their learning at home or to use effective methods to support their anxious times when at home.

However, the benefits for the whole school community continue to grow. There is a culture in our school that recognises and values what AQP can deliver. When the Facilitator goes into each class to collect children, she is aware of other boys and girls asking if it is their turn for AQP, and this is happening on an increasing number of times.

Classes are using the breathing techniques and other relaxation strategies and exercises regularly and creatively, and there is increased confidence in talking about emotional health everywhere in school. Staff members are individually more reflective and also better able to work as a team to reflect on children and help set individual outcomes. Staff members have learned techniques to help redirect children. The whole AQP programme builds trust, confidence and the language skills of professional practice about emotional intelligence.

As a school, we now have pupils, staff and parents who can talk about their feelings and their needs. They can experience and learn ways to relieve stress and anxiety. Parents relish their well-being sessions and want even more. If we did not have AQP, we would have children unable to recognise and manage anxieties, and children who are therefore not ready to learn. We would have children with less empathy, less kindness, less recognition of others' feelings and a lot of relationship issues.

Concluding thoughts

If only every school could have a resource like ours that promotes and supports children's emotional health and development! What a contribution to peaceful schools that would be! We found A Quiet Place and, when it was seen and understood, I knew that this part of our school offer had been missing. It overwhelmingly provides the heartbeat to peace in our school. It does live here, the rooms are full of happiness and love is all around. Even the words 'A Quiet Place' give that sense of peace.

Further reading

Adams, K., Hyde, B. and Woolley, R. (2008) *The Spiritual Dimensions of Childhood.* London: Jessica Kingsley Publishers.

Batmanghelidj, F. (1995) *Your Body Cries for Water.* London: Tagman Press.

Benson, H. (2000) *The Relaxation Response.* New York: Harper Collins.

Buckle, J. (1993) 'Aromatherapy.' *Nursing Times 89,* 20, 32–35.

Day, J. (1994) *Creative Visualisation with Children.* Shaftesbury: Element Books.

Dougans, I. (1996) *Complete Reflexology: Therapeutic Foot Massage for Health and Well-being.* Shaftesbury: Element Books.

Field, T. (1995) 'Massage therapy for infants and children (a review).' *Journal of Developmental and Behavioural Pediatrics 16,* 2, 105–111.

Field, T., Quintino, O., Hernandez-Reif, M. and Koslovsky, G. (1998) 'Adolescents with attention deficit hyperactivity disorder benefit from massage therapy.' *Adolescence* 33, 103–108.

Field, T., Grizzle, N., Scadfidi, F., Abrams, S., Richardson, S., Kuhn, C. and Schanberg, S. (1996) 'Massage therapy for infants of depressed mothers.' *Infant Behaviour and Development* 19, 107–112.

Field, T, Ironson, G., Scafidi, F., Nawrocki. T., Goncalves, A., Pickens, J., Fox, N., Schanberg, S. and Kuhn, C. (1996) 'Massage therapy reduces anxiety and enhances EEG pattern of alertness and math computations.' *International Journal of Neuroscience 86*, 119–205.

Frank, F. (1973) *The Zen of Seeing: Seeing/Drawing as Meditation.* New York: Vintage Books.

Gatti, G. and Cayola, R. (1923) 'L'Azione delle essenze sul sisteme nervosa.' *Rivisita Italiana delle essenze e Profumi 5*, 12, 133–135.

Goleman, D. (2004) *Emotional Intelligence.* London: Bloomsbury.

Greenhalgh, P. (1994) *Emotional Growth and Learning.* London: Routledge.

Hallam, S. and Price, J. (1998) 'Can the use of background music improve the behaviour and academic performance of children with emotional and behavioural difficulties?' *British Journal of Special Education 25*, 2, 88–91.

Hyde, B. (2008) *Children and Spirituality.* London: Jessica Kingsley Publishers.

Jensen, E. (2000) *Brain-based Learning and Teaching.* Del Mar, CA: Turning Point.

Kornfield, J. (2002) *A Path with Heart.* London: Rider.

Kurtz, Z. (1996) *Treating Children Well.* London: Mental Health Foundation.

Lucas, S. (1999) 'The nurturing school: The impact of nurture group principles and practice on the whole school.' *Emotional and Behavioural Difficulties 4*, 3, 14–19.

McKechnie, A., Wilson, F., Watson, N. and Scott, D. (1983) 'Anxiety states: A preliminary report on the value of connective tissue massage.' *Journal of Psychosomatic Research 27*, 2, 125–129.

Mehta, N. (1999) *Indian Head Massage.* London: Thorsons.

Mills, J.C. and Crowley, R.J. (1986) *Therapeutic Metaphors for Children and the Child Within.* New York: Brunner/Mazel.

Montessori, M. (1988) *The Discovery of the Child.* Oxford: Clio Press.

Moon, P. (2013) *The Practical Well-being Programmes, Activities and Exercises.* Milton Keynes: Speechmark Publishing Ltd.

North, A.C. and Hargreaves, D.J. (1997) 'The musical milieu: Studies of listening in everyday life.' *The Psychologist 10*, 7, 309–312.

Olness, K. and Kohen, D.P. (1996) *Hypnosis and Hypnotherapy with Children.* London: Guilford Press.

Piper, H. (2001) 'The response of children and adults to their experience of A Quiet Place.' Commissioned report by A Quite Place, unpublished.

Price, S. and Price, L. (1999) *Aromatherapy for Health Professionals.* London: Churchill Livingstone.

Renwick, F. and Spalding, B. (2002) 'A Quiet Place project: An evaluation of early therapeutic interventions within mainstream schools.' *British Journal of Special Education 29*, 3, 144–149.

Sanderson, H. and Ruddle, J. (1992) 'Aromatherapy and occupational therapy.' *British Journal of Occupational Therapy 55*, 8, 310–314.

Savan, A. (1996) 'A study of the effect of music on the behaviour of children with special educational needs.' Paper presented at the conference of the Society for Research in Psychology of Music and Music Education, Institute of Education, University of London. October.

Spalding, B. (2000) 'The contribution of A Quiet Place to early intervention strategies for children with emotional and behavioural difficulties in mainstream schools.' *British Journal of Special Education 27*, 3, 129–134.

Spalding, B. (2001) 'A Quiet Place: A healing environment.' *Support for Learning 16*, 2, 69–73.

Steiner, R. (1976) *Practical Advice to Teachers*. London: Rudolf Steiner Press.

Sternberg, E.H. (2009) *Healing Spaces: The Science of Place and Well-being*. Cambridge, MA: Harvard University Press.

Wesselman, H. (2004) *Vision Seeker: Shared Wisdom from a Place of Refuge*. Carlsbad: Hay House.

Zohar, D. and Marshall, I. (2001) *Spiritual Intelligence: The Ultimate Intelligence*. London: Bloomsbury.

CHAPTER 13

PEACE EDUCATION FOR A BETTER WORLD

Isabel Cartwright

Introduction

I am the Peace Education Programme Manager for 'Quakers in Britain' or the 'Religious Society of Friends', as it is formally known. I work in our central offices, Friends House, in London in a department called Quaker Peace & Social Witness (QPSW).

The Religious Society of Friends, commonly known as Quakers, began as a movement in England in the 1600s. We are a faith group committed to working for equality and peace. We have our roots in Christianity but also find meaning and value in the teachings and insights of other faiths and traditions. Quakers believe that there is something of God in everyone and that our faith is lived through action. We work positively and creatively with others in order to build a more just and peaceful world. We share responsibility for our work and worship and our life together without traditional structures or paid clergy.

In this chapter, I will first explore the concept of peace education and our approach, referring to a project called 'Fly Kites Not Drones' and how we engage with schools. Second, I will discuss a 'Peace Week' carried out in two primary schools, explaining how it began, took shape, what it involved and the impact of this work. The chapter concludes by looking at the challenges of the society we live in and how and where we should start tackling these challenges. This chapter is Quaker-based, but I hope that it will be of interest and relevance to all.

I am indebted to my manager, Marigold Bentley, for her pioneering peace education work and ongoing support and insight, and to my colleague, Ellis Brooks, for help with this chapter and his limitless energy, creativity and commitment to peace education.

My motivation to do this work stems from early childhood. My mother was a Quaker and, as a Quaker, she believed that all human beings are unique and equal, and that there is 'that of God in everyone' (Quakers in Britain, 2013, 1.02). This belief led her to work actively for peace, seeking the inner light in each person. My mother's peace work took many forms, from working with local asylum seekers to protesting outside nuclear bomb-making factories. We happened to have a nuclear bomb factory at the end of our road and, as a child, I thought that it was quite normal for groups of women to blockade such places and be carried off by the police! As a child, I gained the impression that there is much to be done to make the world safer and fairer, and that we all need to play our part in this.

I am committed to peace education because I believe that our children and young people deserve to be nurtured as peacebuilders. I have a vision of all schools as places where all children are enabled to discover the wonder and beauty within themselves, where the well-being of everyone in the school community is of central importance and where good relationships are considered to be vital to effective learning and development. What is more, I want all schools to be places where children are taught to respond to conflict creatively and where their natural thirst for justice and peace is strengthened.

Society educates young people at best haphazardly and at worst quite destructively as far as conflict is concerned. From an early age, people are led to think that conflicts should be settled by someone in authority. Traditionally, little encouragement has been given to young people to take responsibility for resolving conflicts, to look for 'win-win' solutions (Quakers in Britain, 2013, 24.54).

Our Peace Education Programme seeks to support Quakers, and others, to undertake peace education in their schools and communities. We also seek to grow peace education through research, training, events and conferences, political advocacy, strengthening networks and creating resources.

Building a more peaceful society – the bigger picture

Our understanding as Quakers is that we need to take away the 'occasion of all war', which means to address its root causes. As the former UN Secretary-General Kofi Annan pointed out, a safer world is only a vain hope when conditions are hostile to justice and well-being. 'We cannot be secure amidst starvation…we cannot build peace without alleviating poverty, and…we cannot build freedom on foundations of injustice.'[1]

The Armed Forces currently have a growing role in British schools. This is through such things as the expansion of the cadet forces and the increasing influence of arms companies and the military in Science, Technology, Engineering and Maths (STEM) learning and careers advice.

We believe that there is a danger that unquestioning support for the Armed Forces and British military interventions is being encouraged and war is normalised.[2] Rarely are students encouraged to engage critically with war by exploring the vested interests that profit from war or learning about the alternative peacebuilding approaches to resolving conflict. Where nonviolence is taught, it is usually in a historic sense, for example as an approach used by people such as Mahatma Gandhi and Martin Luther King. We believe that it is vitally important that students are taught that it is also a tool for change today and that it is being used by people all over the world.

Quakers believe that we need to identify the seeds of war in our own lives and educate for peace in the broadest sense. We need to develop the attitudes and values that support inner peace, the skills for interpersonal peace and the knowledge and understanding to engage critically with peace issues from the local to global context. Key to ensuring this is that our schools remain free from militarisation and are places where alternative perspectives are always explored and critical thinking encouraged.

---

1   Accessed 15 January 2018 at www.opendemocracy.net/ammerdown-invitation.
2   The military and arms industries are putting large sums of money into our education system and into STEM educational material for schools. STEM activities are delivered by various parts of the armed forces, and schools are encouraged to participate in military and arms-focused STEM activities through schemes such as the Big Bang Fair and BAE Systems' 'Education Roadshow' (run in conjunction with the RAF and Royal Navy).

So, what is peace education?

In the United Nations Children's Fund (UNICEF), peace education is defined as:

> the process of promoting the knowledge, skills, attitudes and values needed to bring about behavioural change that will enable children, youth and adults to prevent conflict and violence, both overt and structural; to resolve conflict peacefully; and to create the conditions conducive to peace whether at an interpersonal, intergroup, national or international level.

UNICEF's peace education related activities form an integral part of a comprehensive approach to fulfilling the right of quality education for all children (UNICEF 2011). Peace education is underpinned by a simple theory of change and the belief that if this generation learns peace today, then it can build a more peaceful society tomorrow. Indeed, I believe that any peace you see around you exists thanks to peace education whether by parents, teachers, art and culture or experience. An individual challenging racist abuse on the bus, a child resolving a conflict with a peer and a community choosing to care for its most vulnerable members, are all examples of people choosing to be peacemakers because of an educational experience possibly long before the moment of decision. Some peace education is formal and intentional, and sometimes it happens by accident. But it is not simple!

Peace education always has a context. That context will have the seeds both of peace and harmful conflict. Whether in a class, a school, a community or a whole society, you will find people peacebuilding in all kinds of ways as well as people hurting each other. There will be shared norms and behaviours (i.e. a culture), as well as societal structures and systems, all of which have the power to build justice or injustice. I believe that if we accept that the context we operate in is an imperfect 'classroom' for peace education, then it follows that we must also accept that we ourselves share those imperfections. We have been educated haphazardly and we can easily visit that on those we seek to educate. We need to be self-aware and remember that if we are not modelling what we want to teach, then we are actually teaching something else!

Peace education is sometimes broken down into two areas. The first is teaching *about* peace, by which we mean encouraging critical thinking about the root causes of violence and nonviolence and exploring issues such as nuclear weapons or armed drones. The second area is learning *for* peace, by which we mean developing certain attitudes and values for peace such as empathy and tolerance as well as learning skills like listening, communication and conflict resolution.

Another way of understanding peace education is as a spectrum or continuum of activities that include the following:

- supporting the development of inner peace, for example by helping children to be able to handle strong emotions, to calm themselves and to feel good about themselves

- teaching the skills and qualities needed for interpersonal peace such as effective communication skills, the ability to listen to the points of view of others and resolve conflicts before they escalate into violence

- engaging children with peace issues in the wider world, maybe by engaging with peace and justice issues in their community and beyond; learning about the root causes of violence and nonviolence and gaining opportunities to act as human rights defenders and in solidarity with those experiencing the impact of violence and war.

Our approach

Many organisations focus on one element of the peace education spectrum. Some organisations promote mindfulness (inner peace) and others teach conflict resolution skills (interpersonal peace). There are other organisations that engage with issues like nuclear weapons (peace issues in the wider world) such as the Campaign for Nuclear Disarmament's (CND) peace education team.

For us in Quaker Peace & Social Witness (QPSW), our peace education programme works across the whole peace education spectrum. Our approach gives us the flexibility to support the varied Quaker peace education initiatives across the country, which might involve anything from an exhibition or talk about a local conscientious objector in the First or Second World War to a project that teaches skills for peace such as peer mediation.

Our approach also enables us to respond to Quakers' concerns and fill gaps in provision. One example is our response to Quakers' concerns about armed drones.

'Fly Kites Not Drones'

Armed drones represent a new frontier in warfare and, for Quakers, they raise a number of grave concerns. There are high civilian casualties, targeted extra-judicial killings, decisions to kill made half the world away and the possibility of autonomous weapons killing without human involvement. For others, this twenty-first-century form of warfare has huge advantages – principally, that they greatly reduce putting military personnel in harm's way.

Despite the high level of publicity and divergent opinions about drones, there are few education resources that help young people explore questions surrounding drone warfare. Those that do exist tend to explore drones from a factual and technological standpoint, rather than by engaging children and young people with the moral dilemmas connected with drones.

To address this gap, we teamed up with Creative Voices for Nonviolence, who support the inspiring grass roots Afghan Peace Volunteers. Together with other partners, we created a resource pack called 'Fly Kites Not Drones'. The resource pack is grounded in human rights education and we consider how the human rights of some children are denied by living in fear of a drone attack.

The resource centres around the true story of Aymel, a young boy who lost his father in a drone attack on their Afghan village. The resource enables children and young people to consider armed drones from the perspective of civilians living in fear of the drones flying overhead, but also of the politicians relieved by the ability to go to war without risking their troops and also the drone operators themselves. The materials encourage an exploration of positive aspects of Afghan culture so as not to portray Afghans as passive victims or as one-dimensional. It seeks to inspire a desire to empathise and act in solidarity, rather than pity or charity. Hayley Davies, RE and Philosophy and Ethics teacher, and Amnesty International's UK Education Officer, found that 'Fly Kites Not Drones' helped her Year 7s find their voice as active citizens. 'The students surprised me with the standard of their thinking and their desire to actively bring about change in what they saw as unjust. After we flew our kites we returned to the classroom to write letters to our MP, sending all the kites in a call for peace.'

'The students really felt their role as active citizens, using their voices and actions to make a difference to the lives of others. One of my quieter students stated: "This situation is so unfair that it makes me want to keep protesting until something changes'" (Davies 2016).

Our perspective is that engaging children and young people in peace issues, from the local to global context, is about more than developing knowledge and understanding. Nurturing their thirst for peace and justice also involves exploring their attitudes and values. In addition, in order to affect these children, they need to be engaged at an emotional level. Engaging with wider peace issues and taking action in solidarity with others can also support inner peace and enhance self-esteem. It can also support the skills of interpersonal peace if the work involves having to work together in groups, make decisions together and function as a team:

> The practical kite-making element of the resource allows time for more informal discussion of the issues and time to process thoughts and feelings about the issues. My tutor group felt the simple act and enjoyment of kite flying linked them to a group of people whose way of life was very different. The beauty was that the actual construction of the kite allowed for time to process what we'd discussed. (Secondary School Form Teacher)

'Fly Kites Not Drones' has been taken up by primary and secondary schools in tutor time, drop-down days and off-timetable project weeks, supporting SMSC development (England) and linking with various aspects of the curriculum. It is also being used by church youth groups, Guides and Scouts groups.

Taking a broad approach to peace education also enables us to help educators and children to draw connections between the different levels/ aspects of building peace. The reasons for which a conflict may escalate in a playground can, for example, be similar to conflict escalation on a macro-scale (fear, breakdown of communication, listening to inaccurate information, concern not to lose face, etc.) and may require similar support (peer-mediator or playground buddy), just as a macro-conflict may require an international mediation team. It also enables us to help children see the connections between their personal values and decisions, and how this has a wider impact, and to empathise with people – whether their neighbours or communities – on the other side of the planet.

Several years ago, I worked with a group of secondary school students in East London to make a short film exploring the issues surrounding a local arms fair taking place across the road from their school. They could see tanks rolling into the exhibition centre but had no idea why. Through making our 'Where is the Love?' film and exploring the arms fair and the arms trade, the students made the connection between the selling of arms in their community, wars and refugees.[3] As Dr Peter Nobel, former Head of the Swedish Red Cross, famously said: 'Behind almost every refugee stands an arms trader.'

How we work with schools

Our direct work with schools takes place mainly when schools make requests that cannot be met by others. For example, if a school requests peer-mediation training via the Peer Mediation Network, and there are no local training providers, we may work with local Quakers to offer this provision or offer it directly ourselves if we have capacity (we are currently a tiny team of two). We also work in schools to trial new materials and approaches where we feel that they will be replicable on a larger scale.

Having worked in schools for a long time, I can see the pros and cons of engaging with schools as an outside organisation. It can enable a new approach and fresh energy but if the work is to have a lasting impact then the teachers and, depending on what is being introduced, sometimes the whole school community needs to be fully engaged and onboard. For example, introducing a peer-mediation scheme, where a group of students are trained to be on hand to help other students resolve their conflicts, is unlikely to succeed without the support of everyone from the headteacher to the lunchtime supervisors. If it is introduced without this level of support and without some understanding and enthusiasm for developing a restorative culture[4]

---

3   'Where is the love?' is available to watch on You Tube, accessed 15 January 2018 at www.youtube.com/watch?v=KsBOYZk-VrY.

4   In a restorative culture, conflict and tensions are resolved through processes that include all affected parties focusing on repairing harm and strengthening relationships. Creating and maintaining a restorative culture in a school is proactive – it emphasises building, strengthening and repairing relationships and is values-based and needs-led. In such a culture, young people are able to take a lot of responsibility for decision-making on issues that affect their lives. For more on restorative approaches in schools, see *Just Schools: A Whole School Approach to Restorative Justice* by Belinda Hopkins (2003), or online, accessed 15 January 2018 at www.transformingconflict.org/users/belinda-hopkins.

across the school, then the trained peer mediators can be undermined or underutilised and can end up feeling demoralised.

Where schools ask for our support and there is widespread, genuine engagement from staff, and where peace education fits with the overall ethos of the school, then the impact can be huge!

> Peer Mediation has a very high rate of success according to the students who utilise it, with 94 per cent of disputants saying it helped them. Ninety five per cent say that they think mediation makes their school a better place. Staff members report that it helps them do their job, reducing the number of incidents that require their involvement. It has been identified by the Department for Education as the most effective peer support mechanism to reduce bullying. (Hagel and Brooks 2013)

Peace Week – peaceful primaries
How did the project begin?

Upon starting work for the Quakers, I was asked to contribute to a 'Peaceful Primary Schools' conference that we were hosting at Friends House, London, in May 2012. It was an inspiring event. 'Today is about what's possible,' said Anna Lubelska, the conference organiser. The conference was the launch of the 'Peaceful Schools' movement, which seeks to 'bring some stillness and peace into children's lives at a time when concerns about young people's mental health are escalating, children are bombarded with information, advertising and under all sorts of pressure in our global and media-driven society'. Damilola Taylor's father, Richard Taylor, stood up to witness an opening prayer in honour of his son. The effect was palpable. This theme matters. This conference matters.

I was asked to run a workshop. I asked our participants to think about what a peaceful primary school might look and feel like. The group included Quakers, non-Quakers and four headteachers. We explored how you can create the conditions for a culture of peace, talked about the need for children to feel special, heard and loved, and to be given the opportunity to care for others and to feel solidarity. We also discussed the need to work with children around difficult and painful issues like violence and war, and we shared practical resources. We watched 'Where is the Love?' which is the short film that I had worked on with students about the arms trade. The session generated heated debate. It helped me to realise that while many people at the conference were committed to making schools more peaceful places – through things like creating spaces for stillness and mediation – there was less agreement and more unease with the more political aspects of peace education. Yet, surely in order to build a culture of peace, we need to recognise and challenge structures of violence? Children and young people live within these structures – some more than others.

Quakers have historically born witness to uncomfortable truths and kept their eyes open to the many forms of violence around us, and I felt sure that in my new role it was important to stay true to this. At the end of the workshop, one of the headteachers, who had been concerned about the political nature of the film, nevertheless asked me if I would work with her school. She invited me to support her two schools (she was an Executive Head) to plan a whole school off-timetable project week on the theme of peace. An amazing opportunity had presented itself!

How did the Peace Week take shape?

I worked closely with an Assistant Head to plan the peace weeks at both schools. I suggested that they follow the structure of focusing first on inner peace, then on interpersonal peace, and moving on to peace issues in their school and then the local community/wider world. We decided that our objectives included:

- building self-esteem and encouraging a culture of affirmation
- developing communication and conflict resolution skills
- deepening understanding of human rights
- strengthening the sense of class and school community
- deep learning across the curriculum, especially in PSHE
- learning from peacebuilders in the community and beyond.

We were clear that we wanted to deliver the learning in varied, engaging and creative ways and that we wanted to share learning with parents/carers. We ran a whole staff training to engage the teachers with the theme. In the INSET, we gathered staff hopes and expectations, linked the theme of peace with the school values and unpacked the dimensions of peace. We explained that Peace Week would have many parts but that they would fit together to make a whole. Both schools were already regularly using meditation (each day, the whole school community would have a couple of moments of silence – including the office staff), and working on many of the aspects of inner peace. Peace Week offered the opportunity to deepen this work and extend the pupils' understanding of, and skills for, peace.

What happened during Peace Week?

The week involved over 400 peace lessons from Reception through to Year 6 in the two schools! The children examined anger and conflict, played cooperative games and practised mediating a playground dispute. Year 1s made peace books, drawing and describing peace: *'peace is watching the stars at night and watching my granddad shine'*, *'peace is looking after each other and being caring'*, *'peace is making sure everyone has shoes'*. We explored fairness and how different people will have different views about what is 'right' using morally rich stories from 'Talking About Values in the Classroom' written by Quaker author and educator Don Rowe (2015).

Later, the children considered the qualities and skills of a peacemaker and took on the role of journalists interviewing a peace activist, asking questions such as: 'What's the point of protesting at a nuclear base?' Other external organisations were brought in. Amnesty International got the children working as human rights detectives. Pax Christi inspired the children to take their own steps for peace. The Quaker-run Ecumenical Accompaniment Programme in Palestine and Israel used the beautiful picture book *A Child's Garden: A Story of Hope* (Foreman 2009) to explore the impact of the separation barrier on Israelis and Palestinians and discovered the difficulties of getting to school in Bethlehem.

What was the impact?

Staff members were hugely positive about the week. The feedback from teachers and the children was fantastic. 'I loved every moment of peace week!' said one Year 6 student. One headteacher described it as: 'The best thing we've ever done as a whole school community.'

Many teachers brought in additional ideas and resources. They particularly valued support around the less familiar areas of interpersonal peace and international peacebuilding:

> Not only have I learned an enormous amount from Peace Week but also I think it has given me the skills to become a better teacher, to teach children values such as cooperation, listening and how to deal with anger. If other schools could take part in a week like this (or even a few days) I think it would be so valuable to help children understand how to become better citizens in this world. (Assistant Headteacher)

Staff also particularly recognised the value of the children learning to handle conflict more constructively and to consider peace in the broadest sense:

> Peace Week was an opportunity for our children to do some deep learning about critical issues that affect us all. It was time very well spent on the PSHCE curriculum and the children really enjoyed the stories, discussion and debates. The conversations we had as a community during Peace Week will continue to impact on our behaviour and attitudes for years to come. (Executive Headteacher)

> Peace Week has been a wonderful week. It has allowed children to think about their own feelings and emotions and taught them to deal with difficult situations. Peace Week has provided the opportunity to teach children about tricky global issues within a safe environment. (Year 3 teacher)

The materials and approach of these peace weeks supported our subsequent creation of a Peace Week resource pack. The pack aims to support primary and secondary schools wanting to teach peace. We also worked in a secondary school to run a similar week and we also draw on this experience in the resource.[5]

The peace weeks also helped a group of Quakers in Mid Wales who wanted to help establish a culture of peace in local schools. I shared with them many of the materials and they developed a six-week, one-hour a week programme for local primary schools. They sought funding and recruited and trained volunteers. The programme has

---

5   For more information on the Peace Week resource, see: www.quaker.org.uk/our-work/peace/peace-education. Accessed 15 January 2018.

been hugely popular and is operating in around 30 primary schools in Mid Wales:

> The Peaceful Schools Project is an initiative of Mid Wales Area Quaker Meeting, but it is not about Quakerism. It is a response to the culture of violence and hostility in our society, as evidenced, for example, in violent video games and as expressed in bullying in our schools and on our streets. Its aim is to create a peaceful atmosphere in schools where pupils treat each other with respect, work cooperatively, and resolve problems constructively. We begin by establishing ground rules and then undertake very basic conflict resolution work, starting with the individual and working outwards. We cover: feeling OK about ourselves, handling our own anger, being aware of how overlapping and complex are our 'in-groups' and 'out-groups'; then handling bullying and other people's anger and aggression; awareness of different perceptions of situations, the challenges of decision-making and progressing to the potential in cooperation and a more pro-active mediation. Much of the work is done with circle time. We use a mixture of talking, sharing, exercises and games. We use quiet periods and mindful breathing to give pupils the skills to handle their own stresses, and stories to focus attention on particular issues. (Helen Porter, Coordinator, Mid Wales Quakers Peaceful Schools Project)

Reflections on the effectiveness of peace education for achieving a peaceful society

Initiatives such as a Peace Week or 'Fly Kites Not Drones' will not, in and of themselves, develop a culture of peace. They need to be accompanied by ongoing work that supports the well-being of everyone in the school community; relationships need to be prioritised and children need to be given sustained opportunities to act as active citizens, human rights defenders and peacebuilders.

Change takes time, the duration of the career of a pupil in school at least. For society as a whole, we are probably talking about generations. Hence, we witness transforming norms and attitudes towards lesbian, gay, bisexual and transgender (LGBT) rights today compared with a generation ago. Violence used to be a legal instrument of 'peacekeeping' in British schools, but no longer. Tangible change is possible in a shorter time, but it will still be change *within* a context, not transformation *of* the context. When peace education has really succeeded, then the peace in the world around us will not stand out as remarkable because it will be the norm!

The challenges of context and long-term transformation beg the questions: Where do you start? Big or small? Personal or structural? We believe that you should start with an individual whom you know who deals with conflict and invest in developing his or her skills and abilities, and then they might become an amazing peacemaker. Train enough individual peacemakers and maybe they will start to transform not only their own lives but also the society around them. It is a logical theory of change. But how much responsibility can you ask one peacemaker to take for addressing wider structures of power and injustice? For example, training thousands of benefits recipients in mindfulness or nonviolent communication could help them in many ways, but it would not necessarily change the housing shortage or address wage poverty. These structural problems would remain. Equally, if you try to design fair systems without involving the people experiencing conflict and injustice, then we believe that the new systems would fail.

In many, if not all, contexts, peace education is countercultural. The institutions of education can be very authoritarian and competitive, as can society at large. So, in trying to change the world through peace education, you might well be entering into conflict. As with any conflict, the advocate for peace education must choose when to confront and when to compromise. For example, a school might want young people to use restorative approaches to respond to conflict but insist on adults' use of arbitrary punishment. Do you work for incremental change or refuse to be involved on the basis that peace is being undermined?

It is easy to see things managerially when thinking about a school or an education system: 'We will develop systems to manage conflict more effectively.' But in order to transform society, peace education needs to be radical. It needs to do more than act within the system. It needs to transform the system from inside and from outside. In attempting to get peace education recognised within a system of power and control, there is a real danger that it could be co-opted and just become a way of keeping everyone reasonably happy within a society that is not actually very peaceful.

I believe that the answer is unsurprisingly simple to say and fathomless to execute. We need to start everywhere! We should work to educate *ourselves* for peace – being the change we want to see. We should work with individuals to be peacemakers but look to schools to be *communities of change*. And we should be looking at how our whole society legislates for peace. We work within existing systems *and* we challenge unjust systems from without. Peace educators could be receiving a contract to deliver training or could be helping to organise a school boycott of an arms exhibition.

References

Community Speak and the Royal Docks Community School (2004) *Where is the Love?* Accessed 3 December 2017 at www.youtube.com/watch?v=KsB0YZk-VrY.

Davies, H. (2016) 'How flying kites can help teach controversial issues.' *Teaching Citizenship* 43.

Foreman, M. (2009) *A Child's Garden: A Story of Hope.* Somerville: Candlewick Press.

Hagel, S. and Brooks, E. (2013) 'Peace-building through Peer Mediation.' *Teaching Citizenship* 37.

Hopkins, B. (2003) *Just Schools: A Whole School Approach to Restorative Justice.* London: Jessica Kingsley Publishers.

Quakers in Britain (2013) *Quaker Faith and Practice: The Book of Christian Discipline of the Yearly Meeting of the Religious Society of Friends (Quakers) in Britain,* fifth edition. The Yearly Meeting of the Religious Society of Friends (Quakers) in Britain, London. 24.54.

Rowe, D. (2015) 'Talking about values in the classroom.' Citizenship Foundation. Accessed 3 December 2017 at www.citizenshipfoundation.org.uk/main/resource.php?s450.

UNICEF (2011) *Peace Education: I Dream of Peace.* Accessed 3 December 2017 at www.unicef.org/education/focus_peace_education.html.

Organisations and websites

For ongoing work to develop a peaceful culture in your school there are many organisations that can help. These include:

CRESST (Conflict Resolution Education Sheffield Schools Training): www.cresst.org.uk

Leap Confronting Conflict: www.leapconfrontingconflict.org.uk

Peace Education Network: www.peace-education.org.uk

Peaceful Schools Movement: www.peacefulschools.org.uk

Peacemakers (the West Midlands Quaker Peace Education Project): www.peacemakers.org.uk

Peer Mediation Network: www.peermediationnetwork.org.uk

Quakers in Britain's Peace Education Programme: www.quaker.org.uk/our-work/peace/peace-education

Tim Parry Jonathan Ball Foundation for Peace: http://foundation4peace.org

CONCLUDING THOUGHTS

Anna Lubelska

Peaceful Schools – a dynamic movement!

By reading this book, you are already part of a movement. I hope that you have found inspiration and ideas in these pages. To make a peaceful school, there will always be another challenge, but each new peacebuilding step can inspire many more. Each act of kindness, reconciliation and speaking up about injustices that we witness, tells us a peaceful world is possible! When schools nurture those acts, it not only builds peace on the spot, but it also provides a model that can travel beyond the school walls. When we work together to celebrate and share those efforts and learn from them, we are a movement.

The world needs peaceful schools! We need to create an unstoppable flood of peace that will pour out of our schools into our homes, communities and the world! Despite all the obstacles, constraints and frustrations of the education system, I firmly believe that Peaceful Schools will become part of the educational mainstream. Our pioneering chapter writers and many, many others are paving the way for everyone else to follow. The more schools engage in this, the more collective momentum there will be, and the movement will get stronger and stronger.

We have learned that any type of school can become a peaceful school and that anyone can be a peacemaker. We have learned that peace is not a destination but a journey and a personal commitment. It starts with you and it continues through your personal journey, whatever age you are. It has to reach deep into your mind and engage your heart and spirit.

There is no blueprint for achieving peace in our lives and our world. It is an exploration, we have to travel in hope and value all the lessons that we learn on the way. What we have seen is that working to be a peaceful school brings tangible benefits to everyone in the school and can also help with Ofsted ratings. It can help with teacher recruitment and retention and with attracting new pupils. Of course, you need to have at least one or two inspirational and empowering leaders – this can be anyone within the school. Teamwork is vital, as we all know, because together – everyone achieves more!

To become a Beacon Peaceful School you need to have the meaningful involvement of all staff, pupils, parents and governors. Networking and information sharing will bring you more support and help from others. Working in partnership with others, both individuals and organisations, will help you achieve your goals.

To help you on your way you have:

- this book, which is packed full of wisdom, inspiration and practical ideas

- many, many more helpful organisations and publications as identified by our chapter writers and on the peaceful school website: www.peacefulschools.org.uk

- the Peaceful Schools Movement Facebook group

- the United Nations International Day of Peace every year on 21 September, which acts as a focus and a reminder.

Our vision for 2050

Our vision for the future is very positive. We organised a strategic visioning day in the autumn of 2016. The participants included primary school pupils from St Andrews Catholic Primary, one of our Beacon Peaceful Primary Schools. In 2050, the children at our workshop will be in their forties! They are the ones who had the youthful energy and vision to create the following wonderful vision of a golden age.

In 2050, we look around and we can see…

- There is a peaceful focus in the national curriculum.

- There are no Beacon Peaceful Schools as ALL schools are peaceful schools.

- 'Peaceful Schools' have been making pupils strong and believe in themselves, and they will have been spreading unity across the world.

- Peaceful schools will be showing people how to fix their own problems.

- Every school is using restorative approaches.

- Schools no longer have to 'GIVE' young people a voice, because they HAVE a voice!

- Every school is co-led by young people.

- We can see the legacy in the world from pupils who have been to peaceful schools.

And finally...

We leave you with a question: What is your next step for peace?

Index

4P approach 53–5
101 Playground Games (Hoyle) 145
101 Playtime Games (Hoyle) 133
101 Wet Playtime Games and Activities (Hoyle) 133

A Child's Garden: A Story of Hope (Foreman) 209
A Quiet Place (AQP) 188–90
  benefits and challenges 193–5
  concluding thoughts 195
  facilitator 192–3
  feedback 191–2
  introducing 190–1
  reporting 194
'A Quiet Place Ltd' 14
active learning 120
activities of the week 138–9
activity levels 118–19
activity zones 138
adult learning, Peacemakers 71–2
Advent activities 156
affirmation 68, 88
Afghan Peace Volunteers 204
Afritwin project, Woodheys Primary School 170
Alex Hulme Remembrance garden, Woodheys Primary School 167
allotment gardening, Woodheys Primary School 165
animal learning 116
Annan, Kofi 201
Arboretum Trail 165
Ariana Grande concert bombing 170–1
Armed Forces, in schools 201
art, Values-based Education (VbE) 24–5
assessment, peaceful PSHCE 56

Assid, Denise 147
At Least Five a Week: Evidence on the Impact of Physical Activity and its Relationship to Health (DOH) 136
atmosphere, Values-based Education (VbE) 24–5
author experiences 8–9, 19–20, 59–60, 79, 95–7, 133–4, 147–8, 162, 185–6, 200
Aymel 204

Baines, E. 141
barriers to peace 60–1
Basch, C. 137
Beacon Peaceful Schools status 14, 16
behaviour management, playtimes 141–2
behaviour support, inner peace 39–40
behaviour, types of response to 73
Bellamy, David 167
benefits of peaceful schools 12
Bentley, Marigold 200
bereavement/loss support 179
Blackheath Primary School (BPS) 33ff
Blatchford, Roy 19, 141
book
  aims 7
  concluding thoughts 215–17
  hopes for 215
  readership 8
  scope 8
  structure and overview 16–18
BPS 50 37
British Values 162
  peaceful PSHCE 50–2
  Woodheys Primary School 167–9

Brooks, Ellis 200, 207
Brown, Stuart 136
Browning, L. 123
bullying
  approaches to 12, 48
  and prejudice 169
  prevalence 13
  social media 80–1

calmness, activities for 13
Campaign for Nuclear Disarmament (CND) 203
Cardinal Newman Catholic School
  beginnings 176
  chapel 178–9
  concluding thoughts 182–3
  context and overview 175–6
  mission statement 175
  motto 175
  Peace and Justice Group 178, 179
  Peace Charter 180–2
  Peace Garden 178–9
  peace projects 178–9
  Peace through Unity 176, 177–8
Challengers Academy 37
challenges, peaceful PSHCE 57
change, desire for 10–11
child learning, Peacemakers 67
children
  enchanted 161
  as social constructs 9
Children's Safety Education Foundation 168
circle time, Positive Playtime 143
circles for adults 72–3
class reflections 149

classrooms
  concluding thoughts
    113–14
  context and overview 95–7
  creative space 97–9
  looking for meaning 99
  music 98
  openness 101
  outdoor 167
  questioning space 101–2
  space to choose 100–1
  Staffordshire schools
    enquiries 105–13
  see also Philosophy for
    Children (P4C)
coffee mornings 152
collaboration 63–4
Collyer, Cam 118
colour therapy 39
communities, Peace Charter
  182
Community Cohesion 162
community level peace 14
community of enquiry 102–5
Community Speak and the
  Royal Docks Community
  School 207–8
confidence building, outdoor
  learning 120
conflict
  effects of 80–1
  escalator metaphor 70
  as necessary experience 98
conflict prevention 88–90
conflict resolution
  Peace Charter 181–2
  Peacemakers 73–5
consultation 12
continuum of activity 127–8
'Creating a Peaceful School
  Learning Environment'
  (CAPSLE) 12
'Creating Your Peaceful
  School' conference 11–12
Creative Nature Club 165
creative space 97–9
Creative Voices for
  Nonviolence 204
Creators Academy 36
Crucial Crew event 168
curriculum
  Hawthorns School 188
  Peacemakers 63, 75–6
  Values-based Education
    (VbE) 25–6
curriculum opportunities,
  inner peace 37–8

Davies, Hayley 204–5
Davies, Rhys 176
Davison, Dennis 176, 177–8,
  182–3
decision making, pupil
  involvement 38–9
defence, and peace 10

Department of Health 136
Derbyshire Healthy Schools
  48
development of concept 7
drama 69
drones 204
dynamism 215

Easter Reflection 156–7
Eco Schools 161
Ecumenical Accompaniment
  Programme 209
educating for peace,
  Peacemakers 60
education, changes 11
Edward de Bono Thinking
  Schools 39
Elworthy, Scilla 10
emotional intelligence 27–8
emotions, expressing 148–9
empathy 69
  Values-based Education
    (VbE) 27
enchanted children 161
environment, Peace Charter
  182
ethical intelligence 27–8
ethical vocabulary, Values-
  based Education (VbE)
  27–8
ethos, Peace Charter 182
'Every Child Matters' 8–9
Explorers Academy 36
Eyden, Freda 161

families
  challenges to 148–9
  involvement in schools
    152–3
feelings, expressing 148–9
'Fly Kites Not Drones' 204–6
Focus of the Week 150–1
Fonagy, Peter 12
Foreman, M. 209
four levels of peace 13–15,
  46
Frankl, Viktor 99, 100
free play 136
fundamental questions 9–10

Galtung, J. 61
Gandhi, Mohandas 201
gardens, inner peace 37
Gill, Tim 124
Gilley, Jeremy 28
global level peace 14–15
Goh, Jeannine 160–1
Gore, Al 166
Gyatso, Tenzin 10–11

Hagel, Sara 7, 75, 207
Hallowes, Alex 24–5
Hawkes, Neil 20ff
Hawkes, Neil and Jane 23

Hawthorns School
  AQP facilitator 192–3
  AQP feedback 191–2
  benefits and challenges of
    AQP 193–5
  children's needs 186–7
  concluding thoughts 195
  context and overview
    185–6
  curriculum 188
  importance of peace 186–7
  introducing AQP 190–1
  A Quiet Place (AQP)
    188–90
health
  outdoor learning 118–19
  and play 137
Healthy Minds, inner peace
  40–1
Hendrickx, M.M.H.G. 74
Higgins, Molly 180
HM Inspectorate of Education
  (HMIE) 72
Holmes, David 15
Hopkins, B. 64, 206
Hoyle, Thérèse 133, 145
Hughes, Dan 143–4
humanism, Woodheys Primary
  School 169

inclusivity, school grounds
  123–4
individual level peace 13
inner curriculum, Values-based
  Education (VbE) 23
inner peace 148–50
  beginnings 33–4
  behaviour support 39–40
  BPS 50 37
  concluding thoughts 41
  context and overview 33
  curriculum opportunities
    37–8
  decision making 38–9
  Healthy Minds 40–1
  music 37, 39
  Peace Charter 181
  pupil leadership teams 38–9
  safeguarding referrals 40
  school environment 36–7
  school values 34–5
  social, emotional and mental
    health (SEMH) 37–8,
    40–1
  spiritual, moral, social
    and cultural (SMSC)
    provision 39–40
  success and impact 41
  therapies 40–1
  toolkit for 163
Innovators Academy 37
Institute for the Advancement
  of Philosophy for
  Children 101

Institute of Economics and Peace 61
International Day of Peace 28, 29, 166
international evening, Woodheys Primary School 163
International School Grounds Alliance conference 118

King, Martin Luther 201
King's College London 117
Kington, A. 63
Kutnick, P. 63

labyrinth, Woodheys Primary School 166
language
  changes to 27
  conflict resolution 74–5
  relationship building 68
  relationship maintenance 69–70
  relationship repair 70–1
leadership
  pupil leadership teams 38–9
  Values-based Education (VbE) 26–7
learning
  active 120
  adult 71–2
  animals 116
  benefits of outdoor learning 116–18
  benefits of peaceful playtimes 135
  motivation 116
  motivation and engagement 119–20
  Peacemakers 67
  from peers 120
  sense of purpose 99
  sensory approach 99
  teachers' 97
learning agreements, Peacemakers 64–6
Learning for Peace (Peacemakers) 75
Learning in the Natural Environment (LINE) 117
'Learning Through Peace Conference' 12
Lent activities 156–7
liberty 168
link-making 48
Lipman, Matthew 101
Loose Parts play 124–5
Lubelska, Anna 155, 207

Maintaining Curiosity: A Survey into Science Education in Schools (Ofsted) 123

maintenance, school grounds 124
Man's Search for Meaning (Frankl) 99, 100
mental health problems, prevalence 13
Midday Supervisory Assistants (MSAs) 142, 143–4
mindfulness 24
Mindfulness in Schools Project 24
Mindfulness Monday 39
mission statements
  Cardinal Newman Catholic School 175
  practice 150–1
  St Andrew's Catholic Primary School 150, 151
  Unity Group 154–5
  Woodheys Primary School 161
Mizen, Margaret 154
Moon, Penny 188–90, 191
motivation and engagement 119–20
music
  classrooms 98
  inner peace 37, 39
mutual respect 168–9
'My Only Crime' (Higgins) 180

Natural Connections 117
Naturally Inclusive (Robinson and Browning) 123
nature, contact with 119
nature deprivation 161
needs-based learning agreements 64–5
negative peace 61
neuroscience
  brain development 23
  of play 136
Newman, John Henry 175, 183
next step 217
Nobel, Peter 206
normalisation, of war 201
Normandy Day UK 176
Nurture Group 40

Oaklands Catholic School and Sixth Form College see reconciliation meetings
obesity 137
Ofsted, outdoor learning 122–3
Ofsted ratings 12
  peaceful PSHCE 57
  Woodheys Primary School 171–3
One Spirit Interfaith Foundation 162

openness 101
Ord, Will 101
outdoor classrooms 167
outdoor learning
  benefits 116–18
  confidence building 120
  health and well-being 118–19
  Ofsted 122–3
  Ontario study 118
  whole school approach 122–3
Owen, Antony 179–80

parental involvement 152–3
parents, engaging with 162–3
ParticipACTION report card 2015 118
Pax Christi 209
peace
  community level 14
  and defence 10
  defining 7, 186
  four levels of 13–15
  global level 14–15
  importance of 186–7
  individual level 13
  relational level 14
Peace and Justice Group, Cardinal Newman Catholic School 178, 179
Peace Charter, Cardinal Newman Catholic School 180–2
peace education
  defining 202–3
  effectiveness 211–13
  Quaker approach 203ff
Peace Gardens
  Cardinal Newman Catholic School 178–9
  St Andrew's Catholic Primary School 149
Peace Maker certificates 150–1
Peace Mala, Woodheys Primary School 169–70
Peace One Day 29
peace poet, St Andrew's Catholic Primary School 179–80
peace projects, Cardinal Newman Catholic School 178–9
Peace through Unity 176, 177–8
peace trees 38
Peace Walks 154
Peace Week
  beginnings 207
  elements and events 209
  impact 209–11
  taking shape 208–9

peaceful communities *see*
    St Andrew's Catholic
    Primary School
peaceful places 106–7
'Peaceful Primary Schools'
    conference 11–12, 207
Peaceful Project Award 15
peaceful PSHCE *see* Personal,
    Social, Health and
    Citizenship Education
    (PSHCE)
peaceful rooms 14
peaceful schools
    concept 7
    dynamism 215
    next step 217
    vision for the future 216–17
Peaceful Schools Awards
    Scheme 12, 15–16
Peaceful Schools Conferences
    156
Peaceful Schools Movement
    background 11–12
    defining 7
    origins 9, 207
Peaceful Schools Strategy
    Group 7, 11
peaceful values
    context and overview
    19–20
    resources 31
    see also Values-based
        Education (VbE)
peaceful zones, playtimes
    139, 140
Peacemaker Award 15
Peacemakers
    activities and skills 62–4
    adult learning 71–2
    child learning 67
    circle time 62
    collaboration 63–4
    conclusions 76
    conflict resolution 73–5
    context and overview
    59–60
    curriculum 63, 75–6
    educating for peace 60
    learning agreements 64–6
    positive peace 61–2
    relationship building 62,
    67–8
    relationship maintenance
    69–70
    relationship repair 70–1
    restorative justice 73–5
    scenarios 65–6
    skills 68
    SMSC 75–6
    space 62–3
    staff training 72–3
    teacher feedback 76
    them and us barrier 60–1

transformation 73
whole class learning 62
peer-mediation 206–7
Peer Mediation Network 206
peers, learning from 120
Pellegrini, A. 141
people, social need for 10
Personal, Social, Health and
    Citizenship Education
    (PSHCE)
    4P approach 53–5
    anti-bullying 48
    assessment 56
    audit 47
    British Values 50–2
    conclusions 58
    context and overview 43–4
    defining peace 45–6
    drug education 48
    four levels of peace 46
    in holistic approach 44
    making links 48
    Ofsted ratings 57
    outcomes and challenges 57
    peaceful perspective 46–7
    peaceful PSHCE 45
    Religious Education (RE)
    52–3
    and school aims 44
    Sex and Relationships
        Education (SRE) 52
    starting 47
    understanding bodies 48
    United Nations Convention
        on the Rights of the
        Child (UNCRC) 49–50
    Values-based Education
        (VbE) 48–9
    Woodheys Primary School
    167–8
Philosophy for Children
    (P4C) 25, 100, 101–2,
    161
    benefits of 105
    community of enquiry
    102–5
    concluding thoughts
    113–14
    peaceful places 106–7
    Staffordshire schools
        enquiries 105–13
    students' questions 106–8
    students' thoughts 111–12
    teacher thoughts 112–13
    year 5 pupils 109–10
    year 7 pupils 110–11
physical environment,
    importance of 14
Pink, Daniel H. 99
PLACE model 143–4
play
    free play 136
    neuroscience 136
    school grounds 124–5

playground activity leaders
    (PALS) 144–5
Playground Buddies 149
playtimes
    activities of the week 138–9
    activity zones 138
    auditing 137–8
    behaviour management
    141–2
    children's concerns 135
    conclusions 145
    early years and Key Stage
    1 140
    learning benefits 135
    Midday Supervisory
        Assistants (MSAs) 142,
        143–4
    peaceful 134
    peaceful zones 139, 140
    physical health and well-
        being 137
    PLACE model 143–4
    playground activity leaders
        (PALS) 144–5
    problems 134–5
    rules 142–3
    social, emotional and mental
        well-being 136–7
    time spent in 134
    transition to secondary
        school 140–1
    see also Positive Playtime
Pope Francis 178
Poppies at the Tower 156
Porter, Helen 211
positive peace 7, 61–2
Positive Playtime
    circle time 143
    context and overview 133
    see also playtimes
Positive Playtime and
    Lunchtime Training
    Programmes 133
prayer trees 38
prayers, children's 153
promotion of concept 7
pupil involvement, decision
    making 38–9
pupil leadership teams, inner
    peace 38–9
puppets 35

Quakers *see* Religious Society
    of Friends
Quakers in Britain 200
questions, fundamental 9–10

radical examination, of
    schools 8
Rainbow Room 164
Rainbows Bereavement
    Support 179
Rainbows club 149

reconciliation meetings
  beginning 85
  benefits of 81
  conclusions 90–1
  conflict prevention 88–90
  context and overview
    79–80
  control 87
  effects of conflict 80–1
  empowerment 87
  environment 84
  guidelines 86
  meeting style 84
  one-to-ones 83
  referral process 82–3
  role play 89
  staff feedback 93
  stages 83–90
  student feedback 91–3
  use of term 81–2
recreation, school grounds
  124–5
reflection, Values-based
  Education (VbE) 24
refugees 73
relational level peace 14
relationship building,
  Peacemakers 62, 67–8
relationship maintenance,
  Peacemakers 69–70
relationship repair,
  Peacemakers 70–1
relationships
  Peace Charter 181–2
  and Values-based Education
    (VbE) 27–8
religion, as way of life 147
Religious Education (RE)
  peaceful PSHCE 52–3
  Woodheys Primary School
    169
Religious Society of Friends
  approach to peace education
    203
  building peace 201
  context and overview 199
  defining peace education
    202–3
  effectiveness of peace
    education 211–13
  'Fly Kites Not Drones'
    204–6
  Peace Education Programme
    200
  Peace Week 207–11
  peer-mediation 206–7
  working with schools
    206–7
remembrance 156
resources
  classrooms 114
  Hawthorns School 195–7
  peace education 213
  peaceful PSHCE 58

peaceful schools 216
peaceful values 31
Peacemakers 76
playtimes 145
school grounds 131
Woodheys Primary School
  174
respect 168–9
RESPECT values 34–5
restorative consequences 143
restorative culture 206–7
restorative justice 73–5
Reward Assemblies 151
rickets 137
rights and responsibilities
  167–8
Robinson, F. 123
Rogers, Pete 24–5
role modelling 25–6, 71–2,
  73, 176
  Values-based Education
    (VbE) 22–3
role-play 69
Rose, Janet 23
Rowe, Don 209
Royal Horticultural Society
  (RHS) 165–6
rules, playtimes 142–3

Sacred Grove 165
Sadako 163
safeguarding referrals 40
safety
  communities 154
  right to 148
Sandburg, Carl 159
Sargent, Alison 164
School Councils 150–1
school environment, and inner
  peace 36–7
school forest, inner peace 37
school grounds
  active learning 120
  activity levels 118–19
  benefits of outdoor learning
    116–18
  conclusions 130
  contact with nature 119
  context and overview
    115–16
  continuum of activity
    127–8
  designing 120–1
  engagement 129
  health and well-being
    118–19
  inclusivity 123–4
  maintenance 124
  motivation and engagement
    119–20
  observation 126–7
  play and recreation 124–5
  site audit 125–6
  site redesign 129–30

whole school approach
  122–3
Woodheys Primary School
  165–6
zones 128
schools
  Armed Forces in 201
  changes 11
  purpose of 10
Second World War, teaching
  about 163
self-awareness
  developing 22–3
  Values-based Education
    (VbE) 27
self-reflection 69
sense of purpose 99
sensory approach to learning
  99
Sex and Relationships
  Education (SRE) 52
Sharp, S. 135
Siegel, Dan 23
site redesign 129–30
skills
  relationship building 68
  relationship maintenance
    69–70
  relationship repair 70–1
Smith, P.K. 135
social, emotional and mental
  health (SEMH), inner
  peace 37–8, 40–1
social media, conflict and
  bullying 80–1
Society for Advancing
  Philosophical Enquiry and
  Reflection in Education
  (SAPERE) 102
society, vision of 10
space
  to choose 100–1
  creative 97–9
  Peacemakers 62–3
  questioning 101–2
  see also classrooms;
    Philosophy for Children
    (P4C)
special schools see Hawthorns
  School
Spectrum Support Programme
  179
Spiritual England 8–9
spiritual learning, inner peace
  39–40
Spiritual, Moral, Social
  and Cultural Education
  (SMSC)
  'Fly Kites Not Drones' 205
  inner peace 39–40
  Peacemakers 75–6
  Values-based Education
    (VbE) 48–9

St Andrew's Catholic Primary
    School
  building community 156–7
  challenges to families 148–9
  coffee mornings 152
  concluding thoughts 157
  enacting mission statement
    150–1
  inner peace 148–50
  mission statements 150
  parental involvement 152–3
  Peace Garden 149
  peace poet 179–80
  Peace Walks 154
  prayers 153
  pupil voice 151
  safety 154
  School Council 150–1
  School Council mission
    statement 151
  Unity Group 152
  values 157
  welcoming project 152
  Year of Peace 155–6
  see also communities
staff–pupils relationships
    25–6
staff training 72–3
A Quiet Place (AQP) 190
Staffordshire schools enquiries
  classrooms 105–13
  students' thoughts 111–12
  teacher thoughts 112–13
  year 5 pupils 109–10
  year 7 pupils 110–11
stimuli, constant 100
stress 13, 160

Talk Boxes 149
'Talking About Values in the
    Classroom' (Rowe) 209
Taylor, Richard 207
teaching, values 25–6
'The Biggest Risk to Children
    is Keeping Them Indoors'
    118
The Downley School 19ff
The Enchanted Child (Goh) 161
'The Serious Need for Play'
    (Wenner) 136
them and us barrier 60–1
therapies, inner peace 40–1
Together Everyone Achieves
    More (TEAM) 160
tolerance, Woodheys Primary
    School 169
Tomsett, J. 75
toolkit for inner peace 163
transformation, Peacemakers
    73
trees, peace and prayer 38
Tutu, Desmond 170

Ul-Haq, Razwan 170–1
UN Convention on the Rights
    of the Child 168
UN General Assembly,
    Declaration and
    Programme of Action on a
    Culture of Peace 60
UNICEF 202
United Nations Convention
    on the Rights of the Child
    (UNCRC) 49–50
Unity Fortnight 152
Unity Group 152
  mission statement 154–5
unity, in adversity 170–1

value of the week 34–5
values
  British Values 50–2
  communities 157
  teaching 25–6
values assemblies 28–9
Values-based Education (VbE)
    14
  art 24–5
  atmosphere 24–5
  concluding thoughts 29–30
  curriculum 25–6
  defining 20–1
  ethical vocabulary 27–8
  hopes for the future 30–1
  implementing 21–2
  inner curriculum 23
  language 27
  leadership 26–7
  peaceful PSHCE 48–9
  in practice 28–9
  reflection 24
  and relationships 27–8
  role modelling 22–3, 25–6
  Spiritual, Moral, Social
    and Cultural Education
    (SMSC) 48–9
  teaching values 25–6
  transformational elements
    22–8
  whole school approach
    21–2
Values Councils 26–7
values leaders 26–7
values points 35
values puppets 35
values templates 21–2
vision for the future 216–17
vision of society 10

Wachtel, T. 73
Waite, S. 117
Waite, Terry 166
war, normalisation of 201
welcoming project 152
well-being
  outdoor learning 118–19
  peaceful playtimes 136–7

Wellbeing Hub 40–1
Wenner, Melinda 136
West Midlands Quaker Peace
    Education Project 62
  see also Peacemakers
'Where is the Love?' 207–8
whole class learning 62
Whole New Mind (Pink) 99
Woodheys Primary School 14
  Afritwin project 170
  Alex Hulme Remembrance
    garden 167
  allotment gardening 165
  Arboretum Trail 165
  background 160–1
  blueprint for peaceful
    schools 171–3
  British Values 167–9
  concluding thoughts 174
  context and overview
    159–60
  core values 168–9
  Creative Nature Club 165
  engaging with parents and
    governors 162–3
  environmental/conservation
    activities 165
  environmental work 161
  faiths and beliefs 161–2
  humanism 169
  international evening 163
  labyrinth 166
  mission statement 161
  Ofsted ratings 171–3
  outdoor classrooms 167
  Peace Mala 169–70
  Philosophy for Children
    (P4C) 161
  physical environment 164
  PSHCE 167–8
  Rainbow Room 164
  religious education 169
  rights and responsibilities
    167–8
  Sacred Grove 165
  school grounds 165–6
  social events 163
  tolerance 169
  toolkit for inner peace 163
  unity in adversity 170–1
working together 8
World Health Organization
    (WHO) 137

Year of Peace 155–6

Zammit, J. 75
zones
  playtimes 138–9, 140
  school grounds 128